Dr. McBurney's passion for the ‹ pastors shines throughout this bo‹ planning is limned. In *Vital Churches*, you will find wisdom and encouragement that will profit all ruling and teaching elders. I was challenged and convicted.

L. Edgar Barnhill III, Esq., Ruling Elder, First Presbyterian Church of Coral Springs, Florida.

Vital Churches is a valuable guide for elders as they care for their pastors. I am encouraged to see a chapter on the unique expectations and needs of the pastor's wife and family. The examples of challenges that a pastor's wife faces are thoughtfully presented and accurate. Each is accompanied by practical suggestions for elders and congregations as they support and encourage their pastors. This book presents many helpful action steps that can be taken on behalf of pastors and their families.

Mrs. Catherine Metzger, pastor's wife and mother of four children, Pittsburgh, Pennsylvania

In this gem of a book, Wendell McBurney brings to the forefront a much-needed topic to consider: the vitality of our churches' pastors. He astutely understands that it's one thing to survive the rigors of pastoral ministry, it's quite another to thrive. With wisdom and experience compassion and courage, McBurney provides a much-needed antidote to the problems that plague many of our pastoral leaders and their churches. If the statistics are true, too many of our pastors are burning out and leaving the ministry. Moving from the forest to the trees, he provides all the necessary concepts and processes that can help any pastoral leader, along with his leaders, thrive in ministry for the long haul. Every pastor and elder wanting to be faithful in ministry needs to read this book—my students will be reading it!

Rev. Julius J. Kim, PhD., President, The Gospel Coalition Visiting Professor of Practical Theology, Westminster Seminary California, Escondido, California

Many professions are taxing, not just pastoral ministry. But the pastorate has unique stresses that ruling elders do not always recognize as different from the strains they experience in their own careers, or how best to care for their pastor. In this book, Dr. McBurney offers both insight and practical instruction for ruling elders as caretakers of both their pastors and their congregations.

> **Michael LeFebvre**, PhD., Pastor at Christ Church Reformed Presbyterian, Brownsburg, Indiana, Adjunct Professor, Old Testament Studies, Reformed Presbyterian Theological Seminary, Fellow with the Center for Pastor Theologians and author

Vital Churches

Alliance of Confessing Evangelicals 600 Eden Road
Lancaster, PA 17601 AllianceNet.org

The Scripture references used throughout, unless otherwise indicated, are from the Holy Bible English Standard Version (ESV), Classic Reference Edition, copyright 2001, by Crossway Bibles, Wheaton, Illinois.

ISBN: 978-0-9980102-4-3

VITAL CHURCHES

Elder Responsibility for Their Pastors and Congregational Planning

Wendell Faris McBurney

ALLIANCE
OF CONFESSING EVANGELICALS

Dedication

To Pastor Kenneth G. Smith, friend and "Encourager-in-Chief"
to me and many others on matters of elder responsibility,
the vital church and its pastors.

Foreword

*"If we pay the minister that much, it won't be a calling any more.
It will be a profession."*

That comment, which I heard during a discussion on the minister's salary in a congregational meeting, encapsulates the attitudes of many Christians, namely that professional standards ought not to apply in the church. The comment expresses more than the infamous prayer: "Lord, you keep him humble and we'll keep him poor." It reflects the attitude that what applies as good practice in the "real" or natural world, does not apply in the spiritual world. Careful analysis, good planning, and diligent follow-through are at odds with trusting the Lord.

The tendency to contrast decision-making in the natural world with that in the church is what Dr. Wendell McBurney confronts in this very helpful book. But he moves beyond simply challenging this form of thinking to showing congregations and particularly elders how they can go about good, effective planning, particularly for the personal and professional lives of ministers. And I do not know anyone who could do a better job of writing such a book than Wendell McBurney.

Wendell and I have worked together on several projects related to strategic planning and grant proposals as he volunteered his time to help us here at Westminster Seminary California. I have come to count as a good friend this man of remarkable gifts and experience. He is a life-long Christian, dedicated to Christ and active in many different areas in the life of his church. He had long, effective experience at a major state university. He combines keen analytical skills with a good sense of humor. He is definitely someone to turn to for help in planning for the church. And now he has taken his great experience and insight and turned it into a very readable book to guide the church in facing pressing problems in planning for the future and for the ministry.

As I have observed young men entering the ministry over many years, I have seen their professional and personal struggles to settle into their callings. Elders can and should help their ministers, particularly with personal issues like finances and time management for adequate study, pastoral work, family life, and relaxation. This book will be a great encouragement and resource for this work of the elders.

Once when Wendell was with us at our seminary, I opened a planning session with a meditation that I entitled "Strategic Planning: A Reverent Enterprise." (I chose that title because I had already learned a great deal from Wendell!) The meditation was based on Psalm 33:11, "The counsel of the Lord stands forever, the plans of his heart to all generations."

Psalm 33 celebrates the goodness of the Lord to his people, caring and preserving them according to his steadfast love. At the center of this Psalm—which the Psalmist has clearly planned with great care—stands the declaration of verse 11, that the Lord has accomplished all that he has done according to the plans of his heart. The Lord is a planner.

However theologians might discuss the nature of planning in the heart of the One who is eternal and immutable, we should certainly see here an aspect of God that we as his image-bearers are called to emulate. We must be planners. We of course cannot guarantee that our plans will come to pass. We do not possess infinite wisdom. But we do need to recognize that God models for us the call to plan. We must do all with prayer and trust in the Lord. We must recognize that only with the Lord's blessing will our plans succeed. But the Lord has called us to be active and responsible in the life of his church, using the very best of our minds and abilities to serve him.

The Psalmist observes: "The king is not saved by his great army; a warrior is not delivered by his great strength. The war horse is a false hope for salvation, and by its great might it cannot rescue" (verses 16 and 17). The point here is not that kings should not have armies, or that warriors should not be strong, or that horses should not be used in battle. Indeed, we know that David and the kings of Israel had armies, and warriors, and horses. The Psalmist is saying that our ultimate trust and confidence must be in the Lord and not in our resources and strength by themselves. But our faith does not make the careful choice of means irrelevant.

Wendell McBurney, out of his wisdom, broad experience, and strong faith, has given us a most valuable book to lead us in the careful choice of means to serving the Lord through good planning. I am sure that it will be a great blessing to those who will read, ponder, and implement its insights.

W. Robert Godfrey, PhD
Chairman of The Board, Ligonier Ministries
President Emeritus, Westminster Seminary California

What to Expect

Why I have done what I have done

As you read through the pages that follow you will find a variety of topics related to the local congregation and its ministry. At first you might think they are not related, but as you read on you will find all of them tied together by a continuous thread—the need for elders to take seriously their responsibility to provide opportunities for their pastors to develop, use and maintain their skills, remain focused on their ministries and to be strengthened in their personal lives.

The Apostle Paul's letter to Timothy provided leadership requirements for ministry to the church in Ephesus. He was specific about the qualifications for those aspiring to the office of elder, a responsibility he called a noble task (I Timothy 3:1). I have chosen to draw attention to how today's elders, while holding to these same standards, must equip their pastors so that they too can be effective leaders just as Paul had charged Timothy. Some of the suggestions I make go well beyond Timothy. They address some of the challenges faced by elders as they endeavor to support their pastors in the contemporary local church.

Although I have been driven by my concerns for the pastors in my own denomination, I have done what I have done for the broader Church. It is my desire that a new awareness among elders will result in action on behalf of the many pastors struggling to achieve a level of recognition and support similar to other professionals in our society.

This project began while I was recuperating from a lingering illness. Unable to engage in my usual activities, I had a lot of time to think. My thoughts turned to how I might use this unwelcomed leisure in a productive way. Every day is a gift not to be wasted. During this time, I was listening to my pastor's sermon series on the book of Job. I was reminded that adversity has purpose. I soon recognized my enforced rest as an opportunity. It was a gift, a time to reflect on things I have seen, done and learned over the years and how I might use them on behalf of others.

I have watched pastors struggle with overwhelming responsibilities, inefficient use of time, health issues, financial stress, all while their families suffered from neglect. I once helped a pastor drive a U-Haul truck filled with his family's possessions as he moved many hundreds of miles to a new congregation, essentially an escape from an unhappy pastorate. These experiences and observations have underscored my conviction that there is much to be done that can be helpful to our pastors and to the Church.

A pastor who had spent many days working with the elders of congregations within my denomination shared with me his observation that elders often fail to understand the distinction between means and ends—activities and the results of activities. This echoed my own observations and reinforced my desire to do something that would help resolve what I too had concluded to be an all-too-common problem. So, a concern for the church and its elders, pastors and families, combined with some things I have learned, plus some God-given time on my hands, have all served as a confluence of events leading to this book.

Much has been written about the roles and responsibilities of elders. What I believe is lacking is a discussion of how elders can contribute specifically to the vitality of their pastors, and how deliberate action can have an ultimate positive impact on the vitality of their congregations. This book is a challenge to elders, encouraging them to draw up plans of how they will help their pastors with personal needs, the needs of their families and of their congregations.

There can be resistance to planning within the church. It is time-consuming and requires committed leadership. It is hard to do, especially when done well. One of the most insidious reasons for ignoring local church planning is the belief that it is not a proper activity for the church. "God will provide." Actually, God has provided. He has provided the Scriptures that reveal how his own plans have worked for our good. There are numerous examples of planning recorded throughout Scripture. There are reasons for this. We must not ignore them.

Finally, I am concerned that there is an unwillingness by some to recognize the pastor as a professional. I even have heard pastors resist this notion. Yes, it is a "calling," but it requires a similar intensity of academic and experiential preparation, vocational commitment and the same necessity for life-long learning as others including, teachers, lawyers, physicians, airline pilots, first responders and architects.

I once attended a seminar during which the question arose, "What is a professional?" Distinctions were made between some every-day uses of the term "professional" (e.g., "Professional Lawn Care," "Professional Car Wash," etc.) and the typically assumed application of this same adjective to "the professions." Although all in attendance held advanced degrees, no attempt was made to claim exclusive ownership of the term. No conclusive answer to the question was ever reached. Even some thieves are called professional thieves.

One dictionary definition suggests that a professional is a person who is engaged in a learned profession. Perhaps not much help here. I do not have the final answer but will use as my own operational definition to apply to what I have written, "One who has mastered and successfully practices a career responsibility, upholds its ethical standards and has achieved the requisite educational requirements, typically beyond the undergraduate level." I do not propose this as an elitist definition, but one that acknowledges the time that must be invested in learning, and the commitment required of one who engages in a worthy career. I intend this to apply to pastors and to include those pastors who have been graduated by an accredited theological seminary, and thus its applicability to the topics that follow. I address this here only to clarify the philosophical theme found throughout this book. To be clear, I view the pastor as a professional who needs to be respected and treated as a professional, especially by a congregation, its members and its elders.

My goal is a contribution to the vitality of the Church by encouraging its elders to conduct visionary planning for the well-being of their pastors and their congregations. To help me with insights and expertise beyond my own, I have invited two writers to give some perspectives that I otherwise would have been unable to give. They have experienced things that I have not. To them I am indebted and deeply grateful.

Thus, in addressing these topics, I have two objectives:

1. Elders who act upon their responsibility to provide for the personal and professional well-being of their pastors
2. Elders who view congregational planning as being consistent with and exemplified by Scripture

The relationship between deliberate planning and a vital pastor deserves careful attention. This is why I have done what I have done.

WfM

Introduction

How to Read What Follows

This is not the kind of book you will read like a novel. It is very un-novel-like; more like a reference book or topical taxonomy. Even though there is an intentional organizational sequence, starting with the pastor, followed by planning in the church and then by how planning can be used to contribute to a vital pastor, the immediate needs of the reader may lead to some topical cherry picking. This is fine, even encouraged. But there is a thematic thread—elder responsibility for the pastor. Do not miss it.

The life of a congregation concerned for its future will usually require direct participation by some of its members in short- and long-range planning. It is likely that all members will be required to approve any final plan that had been developed prior to its implementation. To do this with integrity requires a commitment to the concept and value of planning within the church. I have included a review of Scripture to underscore both the appropriateness and the justification for congregational planning. It draws attention to some very well-known and extraordinary examples of careful planning. Effective planning within a congregation requires knowledgeable participation, especially by its elders.

A congregation's elders have been given and have accepted responsibility for matters well beyond the more obvious monthly meeting attendance, greeting members at morning worship services and accompanying pastors on occasional hospital visits. Elder responsibility is foundational to the spiritual condition of the congregation. Easily overlooked are some other more subtle yet critical responsibilities. They include such matters as careful attention to immediate and future planning within the local congregation and throughout the broader Church; the need to use great discretion when encouraging members to accept individual planning assignments; recognizing the need for and providing the resources required for the pastor to perform as a professional; and making certain that the pastor, the pastor's spouse and children are each acknowledged as living unique and often stressful lives. Perhaps a game of tennis or an occasional "no-agenda lunch" with the pastor should be included in this list. These are a few of the topics I have addressed, each accompanied by some suggestions. There are many more.

I have been very concerned about the need for the Church to exhibit a greater appreciation for pastors who experience the same and often greater, certainly different, stresses on their lives than others outside the ministry who also hold full-time organizational and leadership positions. I acknowledge that in recent years there has been greater attention to this topic, and it has seen good progress. However, this is only a start.

New opportunities are now becoming available for study and travel leaves, relaxation, self-defined sabbatical leaves and other types of opportunities offering pastors much needed personal revitalization and refreshment. Yet, engagement in these experiences very often requires funds beyond the resources of the pastor or even the congregation. As new funds are pursued, pastors are too often left to go about the search by themselves. Obtaining these funds usually requires preparing grant requests, something with which the pastor has most likely had little or no experience. I have included several items that should be helpful toward this end.

My intent has been to provide some help to the local church as it strives to achieve a vitality that can be elusive. A vital pastor is not the only requirement, but it is an essential ingredient of a vital church. This relationship is intuitive, requiring little more than our personal experiences to be acknowledged. I have included topics that in one way or another, ultimately focus on elder responsibility for planning for the pastor's personal welfare and planning for the spiritual welfare of a congregation. All planning, whether for pastors or congregations, consists of common elements. These elements are explored first within the context of congregational planning, then applied to planning with and for the pastor in later chapters.

If these are topics that have been avoided by a congregation and its elders, likely it is because they are more easily ignored than tackled. I have also included some questions at the end of each chapter to introduce some local reality into what I have written.

The following pages are to encourage, not discourage.

Contents

Elder Responsibility

Planning in the Church

Planning with the Pastor

Planning for the Pastor

Planning for Tomorrow's Pastors

Beyond Planning

Elder Responsibility

— 1 —

Pastor McWeary

More truth than fiction

An introduction to Pastor McWeary will sharpen the focus of my primary concern, the local church pastor. He may appear to be fictional but will be quickly recognized by many.

Pastor McWeary is a mid-career pastor whose family responsibilities now include the demands of one pre-teen, three other children in their teens and another, a Christian college senior. His local congregational responsibilities are steadily increasing. His middle-age health is beginning to show the signs of constant stress. His family has had to be content with vacations limited to annual summer church conferences during which Pastor McWeary and his wife, Patience, have been expected to prepare and conduct the annual youth programs.

Economic pressures are constant. The congregation has done its best to provide compensation that keeps up with inflation but is barely adequate even for routine needs. His compensation certainly does not provide for the constantly increasing cost of health insurance and the bills for his children's higher education, already a burden.

Patience McWeary has remained at home with their children ever since they were born, thus there has been no opportunity for her to help supplement the family income. In addition to her three full-time jobs (caring for her home and husband, raising their children and being their home school teacher), Patience has served the congregation well, assuming the numerous supporting roles expected of a pastor's wife.

Pastor McWeary, now 49 years old, has never been able to attend a professional conference. He has had neither time to keep up on the reading he would like to do, nor to engage in continuing theological studies. After 25 years, the congregation's reward is a weekly sermon that gives further testimony to the reality of professional burnout.

Have you ever met Pastor McWeary? Do you know his wife Patience? Please keep this pastor and his family in mind as you read on.

From Here to Reality

1. In what ways can elders make certain that they are aware of the needs of a pastor's family without unnecessarily prying into the family's private life?
2. How can elders help a pastor avoid the types of circumstances as experienced by Pastor McWeary?
3. What could the congregation have done to help Patience?
4. Does this kind of situation occur primarily in smaller congregations? Can members of larger congregations be unaware of personal pastoral struggles because they are more likely to be less acquainted with their pastors? If you believe this is a possibility, what are you doing to help your pastor avoid unnecessary personal distractions from the ministry?

— 2 —

Attention Elders!

Time to get going

"*On your feeeet!*" *Th*is was what I heard Sergeant Expo shouting at us every morning at 6:00 a.m. He went from one end of our barracks to the other waking up the troops during our basic training. The next thing I knew I was standing at attention outside on the street in front of our Company C barracks. This memory has served me well as a never-to-be-forgotten call to get up and get going when called upon to do so. Right now! No waiting!

This is my charge to you, my fellow elders. Not that I expect you to jump to your feet at this very moment, but that you join me, so together we can "get going" as we consider some ways to be helpful to our pastors—helping to add value to their ministries; helpful beyond the usual elder meeting attendance, assistance with the morning service, response to a call for help moving some furniture or chairing a congregational committee.

I view "eldering" as a full-time job, just as pastoring is a full-time job. This, of course, is in addition to the regular personal employment of most elders. The vows we made when we became elders were not just applicable to those occasions when we are performing our more visible church-related duties. A pastor's vows apply twenty-four hours a day, seven days a week. The vows we agreed to as elders, do also. No difference. No exceptions. And it doesn't end there.

First Timothy tells us that elders are to be above reproach, the husband of one wife, sober minded, respectable, hospitable, able to teach, not drunkards, not violent but gentle, not quarrelsome, and not lovers of money. We must manage our own households well, and with all dignity keep our children under control. We should be neither recent converts nor conceited, and we should be respected even by those outside the church (I Timothy 3:1-7). Our vows are extensive, comprehensive and together they constitute a noble task. I do not view them as time-dependent in any way.

We expect our pastors to be all things to all people and at all times, even on unanticipated occasions: an on-the-spot counselor to an unexpected visitor; a responder to a complicated theological question; or a mechanic when a member's car does not start after the morning worship service. This may seem unfair, but it is more often the reality than not. It is easy to expect full-time duty from our pastors; no breaks, no personal time for themselves, no time off. But what about us, the elders?

Why is it that as elders we find it all too easy to see our roles as applying only to the specifics of I Timothy? Where is it written that our hours of service and responsibility should be restricted to between 8:00 a.m. and noon on the days of our weekly worship services, or occasionally extend to near-midnight on one of those (all too frequent) nights when we must endure a painfully long elder meeting? Somehow, we may see our time commitments differently than we see those of our pastors. It can be very easy to compartmentalize the application of our vows. It may seem easy to remain sober, to not get drunk or to maintain respect in our neighborhoods. But, just as our pastors, should we not go beyond the scripturally mandated expectations of I Timothy, to do the unexpected? I believe that although we had met these qualifications at the time we agreed to assume our responsibilities, we also have an obligation to understand them as being basic to all we do as elders, all the time. I do not view our vows as limitations. I view them as foundational to all we do, and all that we are expected to do, never taking a moment off. We might reasonably ask as Paul did when at the church in Corinth, "Who is sufficient for these things?" The answer is found in the remainder of the same verse. Elders are to be "...as men of sincerity, as commissioned by God, in the sight of God we speak in Christ" (2 Corinthians 2:16-17). God is the source of our strength. There is no reference here to time off.

We expect our pastors to pray for their congregations, including their elders. But do our pastors expect their elders to pray for them? Expected or not, this is a responsibility we have: to pray daily for our pastors, to know their personal needs, praying for the spiritual and physical strength required for each day. I see this as possibly falling under the category of what some might call "other duties as assigned." More correctly, this is actually a normal elder responsibility rather than a specifically assigned other duty. In order to pray effectively, we need to know what to focus on in our prayers. We can only know this if we know our pastors.

To know our pastors well requires a personal relationship beyond the formalities of monthly meetings, once-a-week "good mornings" and the after-the-service-handshake. It requires that we spend some down time with our pastors: an occasional meal in our home; an informal conversation over a no-agenda-lunch at the picnic table in the churchyard; or attending the local high school musical or Friday night football game together. On a number of occasions, I enjoyed a conversational breakfast, and sometimes lunch, with a former pastor at the local truck stop—and some very good food, too. It is amazing how an hour together can expand an acquaintance beyond the superficial. We will quickly learn how to pray for our pastors.

I also believe it is important that we tell our pastors that we are praying for them and that we ask them how we might pray for them on specific matters. This is a way of encouraging our pastors that we must not overlook. It will also lead to opportunities for us to share our own needs with our pastors, thus providing for mutual encouragement and the strengthening of spiritual bonds between pastor and elder. This can lead easily to occasions when we do not just pray for our pastors, but times when we can pray *with* them.

When I became an elder, I acknowledged in one of my vows that I understood that it was "the call of Christ, the glory of God and the welfare of the church" and not any selfish motive that encouraged me to undertake and fulfill the obligations of the office. I suspect that the vows many of you made may have referenced something similar. Emphasis is upon a concern for the welfare of the church as a motivating factor in assuming the office. I have always interpreted the welfare of the church to be very broad in concept. So broad in fact, as to include every aspect of the church. And consistent with the purpose of this book, this includes assuring the personal welfare of pastors within the church.

My challenge is that we acknowledge our responsibility as also including every aspect of our pastor's personal welfare, not just to what I like to call the more obvious "churchie-things." We must include things beyond those normally understood to be the basics of a vital pastorate, often ignored or taken for granted. Things like physical exercise and health, time to read and pray, opportunity for travel, time with family and regularly scheduled breaks from the rigors of the pastorate. It is not enough just to provide a desk, a paycheck and a pulpit!

Every congregation is different. There are those that do an exceptional job of providing for their pastors. And there are those that do not. Some are unable to provide adequately because of resource limitations. Others have the needed resources, but lack vision and the necessary leadership. Leaders, but no leadership! This is a problem.

Much has been written and spoken about elder responsibility for the youth, the sacraments and the spiritual life and health of a congregation. But, generally, we do not hear much about an elder's responsibility for the pastor or the pastor's family. This exception puts the fine point on the issue before us.

During my graduate studies, I asked my physics professor to change my recitation section to another section. I explained that I was having enough difficulty with the physics without having the added challenge of trying to understand it through the nearly impossible accent of my section leader which was producing anxiety beyond the classroom. Dr. Bartis had a firm policy of not honoring requests for such changes, but he honored mine. In doing so, he explained that his exception was based on his belief that one must respect the whole person, not just a student's immediate problem. The relief I experienced left an indelible impression upon me. Since then, I have always tried to look for the less obvious but related issues that might not be immediately apparent when dealing with my students, colleagues and yes, even with my pastors.

I am urging us to view our pastors as whole persons. Not only as those responsible for preaching to us, but as individuals who have emotions, personal needs, hopes and desires, frustrations, families and flat tires. They are like us! We must see them and treat them as having the same kinds of personal needs as we do. And because of their callings, their needs are even beyond our own, unique and occasionally far more compelling. As congregational leaders it is our responsibility not only to recognize those needs, but to treat them for what they can become—impediments to a vital pastorate.

Churches have leaders. But does this assure leadership? I think not. Leadership is the ability to lead others to somewhere other than where they are. But before a leader can lead others to that "somewhere," the leader must know where that somewhere is. The leader must be able show those being led where the new destination is, and why it is a destination to which they should aspire.

We like things to remain the same, the way we do them now. "We have always done it this way." Sound familiar? Why change? It is much easier to just keep doing what we are doing. At first, new shoes aren't as comfortable as the ones we had been wearing. When the "old shoe syndrome" exists in the church it is often unspoken, but just as real as if it had been spoken. When unspoken, our lack of action will soon betray us, often seen as the result of the things we did not do, but should have done. In some form, this seems to be a staple of many congregations. It represents a type of congregational group-think crying for effective leaders if change is to take place; leaders who can recognize a need, define a solution and propose a persuasive plan that will lead to the new destination—the new somewhere. This is leadership! This is how we must engage ourselves on behalf of our pastors if we are to be effective elders. I am not calling for change for the sake of change, but for change in how we view and treat our pastors.

When forward planning takes place in a congregation, if care is not taken, the work required can be easily left to the pastor. This can become an overwhelming and unnecessary burden, especially if planning is done correctly. Good planning consumes a lot of time. It should involve many people; its leaders, stakeholders and those responsible for carrying out the plan. A congregation's reason for existence is to minister to saints and sinners alike. It follows that the ultimate purpose of all congregational planning must have a spiritual focus. The spiritual leaders of the congregation are its pastor and elders. Disregarding the need for elders to be involved is akin to being missing in action—a dereliction of duty.

My challenge to get going requires us to look carefully at how we are currently providing for our pastors. Then we must put together comprehensive plans assuring that we are doing everything within our means to fulfill our responsibility. And if our ways of doing things and our means for change are not adequate, we must make the necessary adjustments to what we are doing, how we do what we are doing, and how we provide the resources required to make it all possible.

Please join me in this incredibly important challenge as we first look at the legitimacy and application of planning within the church, and then examine some matters related to the personal side of the pastorate, and finally some things we can do to prevent that all-too-common, but ever-present potential for pastoral burnout.

On your "feeeet!"

From Here to Reality

1. What are some causes of elder inaction in matters related to a pastor's personal life, especially frustration and stress? Should an elder's busy personal life ever be an excuse for not becoming involved? Does indifference ever play a role here?

2. How can elders hold two full-time jobs while maintaining a credible performance in each? Which job should take preference when time conflicts arise? Does your answer suggest that one is more important than the other? Is it possible that importance can be can be viewed as being primarily time-dependent?

3. Do you agree that concern for the welfare of a congregation must include concern for the welfare of the pastor, too? What should be the relationship between pastor and congregation? Should the welfare of one take precedence over the other? How would you describe the attention you are now giving to the pastor-congregation relationship in your church?

4. What are some reasons why elders should not leave congregational planning to the pastor alone? What difficulties might this produce?

5. What should elders do if a pastor resists elder involvement in planning?

Planning in the Church

— 3 —

The Scriptural Model

Acknowledging the obvious

Scripture is very revealing about the topic of planning, and we must not ignore the message. Strategic planning remains as essential today as it has throughout biblical history, even from the beginning of time. Whether elders are planning for their pastors, with their pastors, or for the future of their congregations, it is important see what the Scripture has to say on the subject.

What follows is not a theological treatise. It is a review of examples from God's Word illustrating how his purposes are the result of carefully prepared plans; how short- and long-range planning is not foreign to the Holy Scripture.

I was once rebuked by a pastor during a meeting of churchmen when I suggested the necessity for careful definition of desired results before deciding what must be done to achieve them. The focus of the meeting was on teaching and learning within the church. I was told that this kind of thinking was rooted in a secular model and had no place in the church.

This pastor is not alone. There are respected people who hold this position. They say that a planning model, which they believe did not have its origin in either the Scripture or the church, should not be applied to the work of the church: The church ministers, but only the Holy Spirit can produce. Thus, they say, man cannot, and must not attempt to pre-define results. My purpose is not to engage in a debate of this specific issue. My purpose is simply to acknowledge the existence of this line of thought. The work of the Holy Spirit is carefully described in Scripture. We see that the Holy Spirit often does work through people.

Examination of how planning has been used effectively in Scripture will give evidence of elements found within each plan that are common to all plans. A synthesis of these elements can validate the Scripture-based model for our use when planning for the pastor or for the congregation. As these are considered, eventual application to our pastors will remain the underlying focus.

Planning in Scripture

We need not look beyond the book of Genesis for our first example. The entire creation gives evidence of careful planning. The first three verses tell us that there was darkness; then God said, "Let there be light;" and then there was light (Genesis 1:1-3). The situation needing to be changed was darkness. Light was needed. God's action creating light followed. The result was light. Thus, there were three distinct planning elements, or steps: defining the existing problem, the condition or need; stating precisely the desired result; and then initiating the action. Note that the desired result was clearly stated before the action took place. Careful examination of the remaining steps in the creation record will show similar relationships among these three essential components of planning.

A second example follows quickly: God's plan to destroy the earth with a flood. In talking to Noah, God clearly defined the problem: "...the earth...was corrupt..." (Genesis 6:12). In the very next verse God states the result of the planned action: "...an end of all flesh." Thus, the problem and the intended solution were each expressed succinctly and with extreme precision within just two verses. Then twelve of the next thirteen verses are dedicated to the specifics of God's plan of action. Of significant note are three things: the explicit statement of the problem; the unambiguous statement of the end result; and a detailed plan of action.

Genesis also reveals another example of careful planning. This time it was a somewhat longer-range plan implemented over many months. It was during the famine in the lands of Egypt and Canaan that Joseph, living in the house of Pharaoh, prepared and carried out a plan to save lives. The situation that needed to be addressed was the coming of a severe famine and the potential for starvation. The desired result was to reduce or eliminate the impact of the impending famine through the availability of sufficient food to preserve human life. A rather ingenious action plan involving the exchange of livestock and land for food and seed was devised and carried out (Genesis 47:13-28). Thus, again, this plan required an assessment of a condition, or need, a clear understanding of the desired result and an action plan that tied the former directly to the latter. The same three essential elements of planning are unmistakably present here also.

An often cited example of planning in Scripture is the military strategy employed by Joshua in the destruction of the Jericho wall. This was a plan that was carried out in only seven days. The uniqueness of the plan was that its success was not only foretold and blessed by the Lord, it was given to Joshua by the Lord. The sixth chapter of Joshua begins by defining the situation as a strong city enclosed within a wall that must be removed. By the fifth verse, the desired result is clearly stated: the wall of the same city flattened. Verses three, four and five describe the plan and the action: men of war marching around the wall, blowing trumpets and shouting at critical intervals. It takes another fourteen verses to describe the precise detail of Joshua's action plan, leaving no doubt about how desired results must first be directly related to what needs to be changed, and only then proceeding to the action that produces the result. A point not to be missed in this record is that the Lord obviously chose to make it clear that a carefully laid plan was essential for producing the results that he wanted for his people (Joshua 6:1-21).

Other Old Testament citations are abundant, including for example, Moses sending spies into Canaan; David establishing his kingdom; Solomon building the temple and his palace; and Nehemiah rebuilding Jerusalem. Each provides a further example of thoughtful planning based upon three interdependent core relationships: definition of the need, a precisely stated desired result and the steps of action required to produce the result.

Illustrations of careful planning are not limited to the Old Testament. Again, we need not look further for an example than the very first book of the New Testament. Matthew provides a fascinating example of Jesus' assessment of a problem: multitudes of people wearied and scattered like sheep with no shepherd; a harvest that was plentiful without enough laborers to do the job; a description of the desired and projected end result required to solve the problem (more laborers); and what had to be done to produce more laborers (prayer to the Lord; Jesus' call for the twelve disciples to join him; his giving them extraordinary powers and sending them to the lost sheep of Israel (Matthew 9:36-38; 10:1-6). The same basic elements of careful planning found in the Old Testament illustrations are unmistakably apparent here also. Jesus sees how the moment is related to the future, in this situation the solution of a problem: how the remediating action must establish a direct and undeniable relationship between an existing and future condition.

The preceding illustrations could generally be considered short-range planning. Today, most plans requiring only one, two, or possibly three years to accomplish are typically considered short-range. However, Scripture abounds with a number of examples of much longer-range planning. The approximately three to five-year plan that Paul made as he organized his travel to Jerusalem, Rome and Spain is a good example of a longer-range plan.

Toward the end of Romans 15, we find a record of Paul's travel plan. Paul had never previously visited the church in Rome, something he had wanted to do for many years. When he had determined that his Mediterranean ministry was complete, he realized that moving on to Spain to start a new ministry would also provide an opportunity for him to stop in Rome on the way. But first he wanted to go to the church in Jerusalem so he could deliver gifts donated by other churches. The apparent complexity and length of his proposed travel required a very careful analysis of needs, desired results and sequence of events or actions.

It is best that some significant details, such as the rationale Paul used for his decision making, be omitted here, thus allowing greater focus on the basics essential to his planning (i.e., needs, desired results, and required actions). It must be noted, however, that the inclusion of these details would serve only to reinforce the planning sequence. Reading Romans 15 will testify to this point.

First, Paul analyzed the situation, describing three needs: a need for his ministry in Spain; a need to visit the church in Rome and to preach "where Christ was not;" and a need to stop in Jerusalem on the way.

Second, Paul wanted to accomplish three things: establish a new ministry in Spain; visit the church in Rome; and provide gifts for the church in Jerusalem (all desired results). And third, Paul's plan included a carefully thought out travel sequence (required action). His first stop was the closest destination, Jerusalem, in order to deliver the gifts. His second stop was to be in Rome, conveniently located on his route to Spain. The timing of his visit to that church was to be appropriate for the ministry that was already occurring there. And after receiving support in Rome, his last stop would be Spain. Again, three classic elements of strategic planning are clear: description of the needs; stating the desired results; and the action required to produce the results.

A summary of the entire book of Romans will demonstrate in a much more general way the application of the same planning components used by Paul: a need for the Word to be heard (the need), receipt of the Word (the desired result), and going and sending (the required action). Further, if God's plan as revealed throughout all of Scripture is examined carefully, we see the same: fallen man (the problem, or need); man's salvation (the desired result); and the birth, life, death, resurrection and ascension of our Lord and Savior (the required action). God is a planner. The beauty of God's plan of salvation is its simplicity.

The beauty of careful strategic planning in the church, and anywhere else, is also its simplicity. The most difficult part may be recognizing this fact.

Beyond its numerous and obvious specific examples of planning, Scripture also contains many admonitions related to planning, leaving no doubt that careful planning is a legitimate part of God's own plans. For example, Acts 4 reminds us to pray for boldness in carrying out plans, as Peter and John did following their arrests. Sometimes our plans are not God's plans as we are reminded in I Chronicles 28, when God told David that he was not to use the plans he had given him for building the temple, but to turn them over to Solomon. We are warned in Proverbs 21:30, that God's plans will always prevail, not the plans of man. Other references to plans and planning are found throughout the book of Proverbs. Further exegesis is not my intent; defining the Scriptural model is.

In addition to the "three basics" apparent in each of the preceding examples from Scripture, there is a requisite understanding essential to their meaningful application to any plan. First, we see that it was essential in each situation to be changed or eliminated, that the need was clearly understood and carefully defined. Second, the desired result of every proposed plan of action was stated before the action began. Third, each step of an action was directly related to the original situation and to the desired result. The action formed a "bridge" between the need and the result. And finally, there was in each situation an unequivocal recognition of the distinction between actions (means) and desired results (ends), something all too often ignored in contemporary church planning. Means must not be confused with ends. There are other less obvious, more technical specifics that can be gleaned from an expanded analysis and synthesis of planning as found throughout the Scriptures, however they are not necessary here.

It should not be missed that these planning basics are consistent with those commonly found in many of today's business plans. This should raise the question: which came first, the Scripture model or the contemporary business (secular) model? The answer should be clear, suggesting that we should not always fear what we find around us when it might be helpful. This is especially true when, as in this case, we find principles consistent with, and conceivably even derived from, principles found in Scripture. Although the derivation may not be easily or ever confirmed, the chronological relationship and the precedent is clear.

A critical ingredient of strategic planning is the proper and necessary sequence of steps in the planning process. As with any action, first things must come first. At the beginning of any plan it is important to be clear about two things: the existing conditions to be changed or eliminated, and the conditions desired after the plan has been completed. Only then can it be determined what must be done to turn the existing situation into the new situation. Note the sequence. The first two steps must precede the action. Therein lies one of the most commonly abused concepts of strategic planning. Too often the action is decided before the desired results have been carefully addressed, or even before the need is defined. I find it amusing when the PTA holds a fundraising event to benefit the local elementary school, and only after the event is over, meets to figure out how to spend the money. (See ch. 7, The Planning Sequence.)

Of special note is that the plans recorded in Scripture are all, in one way or another, related to people and to the ultimate ministry of Christ on earth, thus the church. It is not unreasonable to assume that the planning principles observed throughout Scripture can be applied directly to the contemporary church as well. Thus, elders must not be afraid to look for ways to apply them within our congregations.

Application to the Church

How often do we see a church activity conducted because it is a "good thing to do" (the action) before a precise understanding of the desired results have been carefully thought out? The answer: too often. Relate this question to Bible school classes, elder and congregational retreats, Vacation Bible School, etc.

It is easy to invite Pastor Delectate to address young people during a summer conference because he is a great speaker and he identifies well with youth. Indeed, he may be an engaging speaker and goes over well with the teens. But it is essential, in order for him to be truly effective, that Pastor Delectate be advised of the specific expectations planners have for what needs to be accomplished by his presentation. What is it that the teens should know by the time the address is over, that they didn't know when they arrived? Or what should they be able to do, that they could not have done before his talk? What need will have been served or eliminated?

This should be a concern of the speaker also. For example, an invited speaker should ask, "What are the needs of the group to which I will be speaking?" "What would you like my comments (actions) to accomplish (results)?" "What are your expectations?" Recall that when Paul spoke at Corinth, he first acknowledged the condition of the church (divisions among the members) and what the results should be (a church unified "in the work of the Lord"). He then knew what to say and how to say it (I Corinthians 1:10 and 15:58). The Scripture model suggests that initial planning should first assess and carefully define the specific needs of the intended audience. Then the desired responses to the message should be clarified, and finally, a qualified speaker should be engaged and properly equipped with this information. Only then will the speaker be able to provide a bridge between a group's needs and the expectations of how the group will be changed. Note, again, that the action (the actual speaking) comes last. Response to the message follows.

These same or similar concerns, are essential to all planning within the church whether it is teaching a Bible school class, planning a congregational retreat, conducting a Vacation Bible School, and yes, even planning for a pastor's sabbatical. Typically, it is rather easy for the Facilities Committee to recognize the need for defining the "before" and "after" if it is preparing plans for an addition to the church building. However, the same type of careful planning applied to a construction project should also apply to congregational programs and pastoral care. In both, careful planning requires that the existing situation be contrasted with the final condition or expectation, so the proposed activity will directly relate the two. That is, if the "before" condition is to be replaced by the "after" condition, the change must be caused by an activity that unites the two.

Does this model also apply to the conduct of congregational committee meetings? Yes! It should apply when setting agendas for any meeting. For example, it should be used when the elders decide to hold a congregational retreat for the purpose of helping committee leaders become more effective in their future program planning efforts. It is easy to hold such an event without first deciding exactly what the expectations are, beyond hopefully hearing something new. What will be expected of the chairs of the Mercy and Missions Committees, or of each Bible school teacher? What skills are they presently lacking? What new skills do they need? Should the expectations be the same for each leader? Will the retreat just be the "same old, same old," with attendees coming just because they are expected to come and listening because they should? Or will attendance result in the acquisition and use of new skills directly applicable to specific congregational responsibilities? If no new expectations exist, why hold the retreat? If such expectations do exist, have the retreat speakers been carefully informed so their contributions will establish the necessary bridge between needs and expectations? If not, the purpose of the retreat could come perilously close to holding a retreat simply for the purpose of holding a retreat, not unheard of in the church. Doing something is not a reason for doing something.

We must not be afraid to make plans, fearing that our plans may not be in accord with God's plan. God will change them if he chooses. Remember what God told David when he wanted to build a temple. If this happens to us, our response must be the same as David's. We must respond accordingly. We will find out soon enough if it is not God's plan to proceed. James 4:15 states that, "If the Lord wills, we will live and do this or that." Genesis chapter 11 reminds us not to forget the tower that some intended to reach the heavens. However, there is no purpose in just sitting around waiting for a specific signal from heaven before engaging in congregational planning. This signal, or directive, was already accepted when our elder responsibilities were assumed. If we wait for lightning to strike, we will fail.

In all planning, we must first seek the Lord's approval. We must be as confident as Job was when he confessed to the Lord, "I know that you can do all things; no plan of yours can be thwarted" (Job 42:2). We must pray for the wisdom we need, and for his guidance. While engaging in the planning activities of our congregations, we must always look through the eyes of our faith. Hebrews chapter 11 tells us, "Now faith is the assurance of things hoped for, the conviction of things not seen." In no way should planning take the place of our faith. It must be a demonstration of our faith.

A portion of a metric version of Psalm 139 expressed in Old English that is sung in worship services is appropriate here. It reminds us that God knows the plans we make, even before we do.

Lord, thou hast searched me; thou hast known
My rising and my sitting down;
And from afar Thou knowest well
The very thoughts that in me dwell.

Thou knowest all the ways I plan,
My path and lying down dost scan;
For in my tongue no word can be,
But, lo, O Lord, 'tis known to Thee.

Behind, before me, Thou dost stand
And lay on me Thy mighty hand;
Such knowledge is for me too strange
And high beyond my utmost range.

The Book of Psalms for Singing; © 1973
Reformed Presbyterian Chuch of North America

In summary: The Holy Scriptures provide numerous examples of how careful planning was integral to God's own plan for the salvation of mankind. Other examples throughout Scripture clearly illustrate principles that can be applied directly to strategic planning by elders in our congregations. Accordingly, a successful plan must first include a careful assessment of the moment. That is, whatever it is that needs to be changed or eliminated must first be determined. Next, a clear and accurate description of desired results or outcomes must be defined. Only then can a plan of action that forms a bridge directly linking the need and the results be realistically prepared and successfully implemented.

Successful congregational planning is dependent upon prayer and a desire to move ahead with full confidence in God's leading and oversight. Strategic planning in the church is an ever-present responsibility of elder leadership. It is an example of faith.

> *"...which of you, desiring to build a tower, does not first sit down and count the cost, whether he has enough to complete it? Otherwise, when he has laid a foundation and is not able to finish, all who see it begin to mock him, saying, 'This man began to build and was not able to finish'"* (Luke 14:28-30).

From Here to Reality

1. Should a congregation look to "outside" sources for examples of well-run organizational models? To what extent should a congregation be organized for functional efficiency? Can a congregation be "over organized?" If so, how could this happen? Are there dangers?

2. Do examples of good planning found in Scripture always translate into applicable models for the church?

3. What can be the cause of congregational activities being planned and carried out without the necessary attention to desired results?
4. Are the results of programs run by your congregation ever evaluated to determine the degrees of success achieved? Or lack of success?
5. What is success in the church?
6. Is it appropriate to evaluate the success of our congregational planning, especially when spiritual matters are involved?

— 4 —

Prayer that Permeates

Diffusion and submission

A scientific reality I learned years ago was how some substances pass through permeable membranes and other barriers. It has never left me. My dictionary defines "permeable" as being "capable of being permeated," or allowing diffusion to occur. "Permeate" is defined as "to spread or diffuse through." I don't believe it is unreasonable to apply this same concept to planning and prayer, as prayer must permeate every aspect of our lives. In the context of the preceding and following chapters, prayer must permeate or diffuse throughout all of our planning. Planning must also be permeable to our prayers.

Beginning and ending every meeting with prayer, regardless of the meeting's purpose, has become an expectation and common practice on many church-related occasions. I'm neither advocating nor discouraging this practice. I am, however, urging that all planning be accompanied—even permeated—by prayer. A universally applicable prescription for time or place of prayer is not possible. What is possible, however, is for elders to encourage a clear and necessary understanding of the relationship between good planning and prayer. Prayer must be an integral component of planning, diffusing through each step of the process.

All planning must acknowledge and be submissive to the sovereignty of God. Prayer is an act of submission to his will. It is a means of seeking his will and not merely pressing ahead with our own. The will of God includes the things he has decreed from eternity. Bringing our plans to him in our prayers is our way of determining their compatibility with his eternal plan.

Jeremiah the prophet has recorded a remarkable call for elders to seek God's plan when he addressed them about their Babylonian exile.

"For I know the plans I have for you declares the Lord, plans for wholeness and not for evil, to give you a future and a hope. Then you will call upon me and come and pray to me, and I will hear you. You will seek me and find me, when you seek me with all your heart. I will be found by you, declares the Lord..." (Jeremiah 29:11-14) This message to elders is as applicable today as it was then.

Engaging in prayer during every phase of congregational planning will be an acknowledgment of our dependence upon God. When we pray, "Thy will be done," in the Lord's Prayer, we are stating our obedience to the will of God. As plans are developed and carried out for congregations, elders must be assured of God's will, and that plans being developed are consistent with God's plan for the visible church. Acting in response to this assurance will be an expression of our submission.

Not to be overlooked is the need to plan for prayer; not just the need to pray for a plan. Proverbs 19:21 tells us that, "Many are the plans in the mind of a man, but it is the purpose of the Lord that will stand." The priority is clear. His purpose must be found throughout all planning — it must permeate. Thus, it is wise to think through the various steps required during any planning process: the organizational meeting, assessing and defining the need, determining goals and objectives, putting together the action plan, and after obtaining the various reviews and necessary committee and elder approvals, presenting the final plan to the congregation. Each step will involve unique issues and challenges. Some can be anticipated, others cannot. However, opportunity exists for anticipating some of them, and aligning prayer topics with each phase and need. This can be done by monitoring progress carefully and relating it to prayer topics in the form of a planning-progress calendar. This will require periodic attention to the dynamic nature of progress. The focus of supporting prayer will then be continuously updated.

Once a planning-progress calendar is in place, an accompanying plan for supporting prayer can be determined. This is a good opportunity for elders to exhibit leadership in matters of congregational prayer. They can prepare the topical prayer assignments on behalf of those who will be engaged most directly in the planning process, even making prayer assignments for themselves. Prayer opportunities need not be reserved solely for the more formal meetings associated with planning, but should also include informal supporting prayer groups, families and individuals. The prayer calendar can be distributed to all members of the congregation electronically, or even accompany the printed weekly worship program.

Again, the "where and when" of prayer needs to be determined locally. But the need to assure that opportunity for prayer is diffused throughout a planning process is universal, and not just a local matter. It is always present, never to be ignored.

From Here to Reality

1. How should what may appear to be "unanswered prayers" influence planning in the church?

2. What can elders do to encourage a meaningful relationship between congregational planning and prayer?

3. Consider what can become impediments to incorporating prayer within the planning process, suggesting ways elders can help the congregation avoid them.

4. Jeremiah's call for elders to seek God's plans for them is just as applicable today. What are some practical ways for elders to heed this call while planning in the church? Is this being done in your congregation?

— 5 —

Some Planning Proverbs

Planning for planning

Many things can be said to encourage good planning in the church. Throughout his book, *Strategic Planning for Christian Organizations: Turning The Power of Vision Into Effective Ministry*, Dr. Guy Saffold has been particularly insightful in addressing the topic. With his permission, some references have been gleaned from his work and presented below as "planning proverbs."* Several have been slightly edited.

- Someone will occasionally object to planning on the grounds that if we truly follow the leading of God's Spirit, we will have no need for planning. "The Lord will guide us day by day," is the sincere but mistaken expression of this view. If plans were unnecessary, why would God have provided David with the details for the temple, and why would David have committed them to writing?
- For Christian believers, strategic planning is never an attempt to replace faith but rather to express it.
- Strategic *thinking* is more important than strategic *planning.*
- The more significant the opportunity, the greater the barriers.
- Leaders who do not devote a major share of their time to thinking about the future are failing to lead.
- The point of planning...is not to predict what will happen, but to envision what God wants to do and then lay the very best plans possible to achieve that vision.
- Strategic thinking recognizes that external realities are almost always beyond one's control, and the pressures they generate cannot be ignored.
- Strategic thinking recognizes that, in the end, it is impossible to maintain the existing status...

- Few Christian organizations face the danger of over-planning.
- It is somewhat refreshing to discover that many strategies suggest that the best strategic plans are often remarkably simple. The insight and creativity of a plan are more important than its length.
- Strategic planning is likely to prove valuable only when a conscious effort is made to ensure that it begins with the best quality strategic thinking your organization's leadership can generate.
- Strategic planning can be especially time consuming because it presses leaders to examine basic assumptions, to question current directions, and to consider major alternatives for the future...
- We had better recognize at the outset that the mere fact of being Christian is no guarantee of survival.
- "If you don't know where you're going, you might end up somewhere else." (Casey Stengel)
- The process that leads up to preparation of the plan is more important than the document itself.
- Belief in an unchanging theology can almost unconsciously become belief in unchanging organizations, a very serious error.
- The most effective cultures support rather than discourage change.
- Strategic planning is a tool for effective adaptation to change while preserving values that should not change.
- Resistance to change arises naturally, but forging new patterns is hard work.
- Producing adaptive change in the service of timeless values is the true work of...leadership.
- Strategic planning is based on the development of a clear understanding of mission or purpose.
- Will the organization's current direction...move it toward its strategic objectives?

- The best strategic planning is done by people who are passionately involved with the organization and have deep, personal convictions about what it should be and do.
- Strategic planning requires clear, logical discussion, but it succeeds also to the degree that leaders are able to tap into their true feeling and intuitions about what is right for the organization.
- Discussions about basic values, allocation of scarce resources, and ultimately, the acceptance of some proposals and the rejection of other proposals are often deeply emotional dialogues that may involve strong feelings and even heated debate. All of these things are part of the strategic planning process.
- Planning techniques and the exercise of faith need never be at odds.
- A clear, unambiguous signal from senior leaders is needed to communicate that the planning process is important and its results will be taken seriously.
- In strategic planning, the first major step is to clarify mission.
- A razor sharp focus on the end result is the most important characteristic of a good mission statement.
- A surprisingly common error is a mission statement written in terms of the process, or the means used to achieve the results, rather than in the terms of the results themselves.
- Strategic planning is more intuitive than analytical.

**Used with the written permission of Dr. Guy S. Saffold, author of Strategic Planning for Christian Organizations; originally published by the Accrediting Association of Bible Colleges (now the Association for Biblical Higher Education); © 1994.*

From Here to Reality

1. If "the greater the need for congregational planning, the greater the problems to be anticipated" is true, are there ways to avoid this? Who is responsible?

2. Is predicting the outcome of good planning compatible with seeking God's will?
3. Is it possible for a congregation to do too much planning?
4. What are some of the greatest challenges experienced by elders who are responsible for congregational planning?
5. Should there be a difference between planning for the spiritual life of a congregation and other types of congregational planning (e.g., financial, social, organizational, etc.)?
6. What are some of the first steps elders should take when engaging the congregation in the planning process?

— 6 —

Mission and Ministry

The North Star of purpose

Numerous Scripture references speak to the church and its purpose, including Acts 2:42; Matthew 28:18-20; Acts 20:28; Matthew 18:15-20; and I Corinthians 12:12-28. Ephesians 4 declares the church as the body of Christ, with verses 11, 12 and 16 stating how Christ gave to the church *"...the apostles, the prophets, the evangelists, the pastors and teachers to equip the saints for the work of the ministry, for building up the body of Christ..."* and that the body is *"...joined and held together by every joint with which it is equipped, when each part is working together properly, makes the body grow so that it builds itself up in love."* Unmistakably, the relationship between the church and its people is obvious and direct. It is also clear that for the church to grow, each part of the church must work "together properly."

A congregation's mission statement is a means of making a commitment to assure that each part of the congregation is working together properly, and is focused upon the same purpose—the glory of God. A clear statement of congregational mission is of much greater value than any goal or objective. It is more global. It states where the congregation's efforts will be concentrated as it carries out its role in "building up the body of Christ." It is the most essential element of planning. The congregation's mission statement is its "North Star," something to be consulted as a guide every time a plan or other related decision is being made. It will keep the congregation on course.

But beware! A mission statement can be boring. It can be too long. It can lack interest. Worst of all, it can be ignored. There is a reason for each of these faults. A mission statement can be boring because it is too wordy, too rambling, neither generating nor holding interest. It can be too long because it includes too many unnecessary details, is not focused. It can lack interest because it lacks creativity. It can be ignored by a congregation because the members just don't want to be bothered by such a thing, or they may not even know it exists.

Unfortunately, the essential link between a congregation's mission and its ministry can be too easily ignored, although perhaps not intentionally. Any attempt to define the relationship, if done properly, takes considerable thought and time. It may even be viewed as unnecessary because "everyone knows what the relationship is; it is too obvious to be worth the effort to prepare an actual written statement of our mission." Wrong!

So, what is a mission statement? This may depend upon who one talks to, or what one reads. There are numerous examples out there. I propose the following operational definition for a congregation's mission statement: *A brief, general statement summarizing a congregation's purpose, capable of being supported by one or more goals and objectives.* That is it. Simple, yet challenging. This definition is consistent with the terms, "goals" and "objectives" and planning in general as used in the following chapters. (See ch. 9, Goals Versus Objectives.)

Relationships among an objective, a goal and a mission are sequential. Specificity deceases as we progress from an objective to a mission. That is, a stated objective although brief, should be as specific as possible. A stated goal is more general. A mission statement is even more general, more global.

Much could be said about the characteristics and content of a congregation's mission statement, yet again, a simple approach is best. The statement should be brief, comprehensive, consistent with all supporting goals and objectives, establish a compelling relationship between the congregation and the reader and serve as an effective and realistic guide to all planning. The most challenging part of this will likely be the need for brevity.

The most effective mission statement will be no longer than one, two or possibly three sentences; preferably just one. And certainly, no more than one paragraph. It will take great care and effort to condense the requisite global nature of the statement into one or two sentences. This is the hard part. It can be frustrating and unexpectedly time consuming.

Hint: the first step toward composing a mission statement is best attempted by only one individual, not a committee. Only then should a draft be shared with a small group or committee for comment and refinement. This will save a great amount of time and contested conversation. The more people who are included in the early planning stages, the more complex and time-consuming the assignment will become. This is not unlike my recommended approach to any other planning effort.

Examples of two mission statements are presented below; the first for a congregation, the second for a committee.

1. The First Church of the Anointed is committed to reaching the lost through Scripture-based ministries.

2. Churches Alive is a committee of the Church of the New Creation functioning as a catalyst to promote effective congregational leadership resulting in spiritually healthy lives.

Examination of these two illustrations reveals the following most basic characteristics of a mission statement.

1. Brevity

2. The name of the congregation or committee

3. What the congregation or committee does (conducts Scripture-based ministries; promotes effective congregational leadership)

4. The ultimate purpose (reaching the lost; spiritually healthy lives)

It is occasionally recommended that a mission statement be accompanied by a vision statement. Typically, a vision statement is one that is even more global (or visionary) than the mission statement. It attempts to "see" beyond the mission. It describes the desired future. Whereas it may be difficult to prove that a mission has ever been achieved (other than progress toward it), it will be more difficult, and nearly impossible to prove anything more than that a vision exists. This reality is often overlooked when planning. It should not dissuade planners from recognizing that all planning is a means of working toward an ultimate future.

In the two examples above, the second one may come closer to incorporating a reference to the future. It projects spiritually healthy lives as its vision. The first example includes no specific reference to an ultimate vision. A further reference to what "reaching the lost" might accomplish would be visionary.

The technical and definitional distinctions required to distinguish between mission and vision can present unprofitable and time consuming challenges to church planning. It has the potential to discourage and distract from focusing on what is most essential, setting the "North Star." My recommendation is to restrict planning to the use of only a mission statement. However, the possibility of incorporating the essence of vision within the mission always exists and can be very desirable. This decision should be made as circumstances dictate and time permits. It may require an additional sentence or two, but this will be fine if the rule for brevity is respected.

The worst possible fate for a mission statement, regardless of how well it has been crafted, is to have it languish in an electronic file or in a folder hidden somewhere in a file cabinet. I recommend that it be prominently but judiciously displayed in places where it will be most helpful to the most people. This can include being printed at the beginning of the agenda for every meeting of the elders and every committee meeting, and even the agenda for each congregational meeting. Including it in the program for the weekly worship service will be a good reminder to members and be informative to visitors. If it is as brief as recommended, it will consume only minimal space.

Keep the mission statement out of the file.

From Here to Reality

1. Which is of greater importance: taking the time to first establish a mission statement before solving immediate needs, or moving ahead to address current and urgent circumstances without benefit of a clearly defined mission? How should you respond to other elders who may not agree with your view? What kind of problems can be encountered when setting mission related priorities?

2. What is the relationship between an objective and the mission?

3. How can a mission statement be both brief and comprehensive? Try preparing one that is no longer than three sentences for use by a committee on which you serve.

4. Providing no more than five minutes, have each elder in your elder group independently prepare a draft mission statement for your congregation. Upon completion, have each elder critique another's draft, using the criteria recommended. Was preparing the mission statement easy? How could it have been easier? What was learned?

5. What is the greatest danger that can be encountered by a congregation's mission statement?

6. Is it responsible for a congregation's mission to remain ill-defined, given the many clear examples of the mission of the Christian Church found throughout Scripute (e.g. Matthew 28:18–20; I Corinthians 1:2)?

— 7 —

The Planning Sequence

Means versus ends

There are three questions that need to be asked when preparing a plan: what needs to be changed; what results are desired; and what will bring about the change? Interestingly, these are the same components of plan implementation. The only difference is the sequence in which they should be considered. This point can be missed, especially in the early stages of planning.

When *creating* a plan, the contrast between the need and the objective(s) must be established *before* the action required to achieve the change can be accurately determined. When *implementing* the same plan, this sequence changes. The action must then precede the objective(s). That is, the action will produce the objective(s).

When putting a plan on paper, stating the desired objective(s) immediately following the stated need will emphasize the contrast between them. The dissonance will contribute toward clarifying the action required. This will help those who prepare the plan, those who read the plan and those who carry out the plan. (See ch. 22, Preparing a Request.) The following representation may be helpful:

When Planning

Step 1		**Step 2**		**Step 3**
Need	→	Objective(s)	→	Action

When Implementing a Plan

Step 1		**Step 2**		**Step 3**
Need	→	Action	→	Objective(s)

Without a clear understanding of these relationships, congregational planning can be ineffective. It can contribute to failed leadership. It is easy to make plans focusing primarily on what is to be done, giving less attention, or no attention at all, to what is to be accomplished. For example, consider how easy it can be for elders and pastors to plan a sermon series based upon which topics have not been preached upon lately, without giving much thought to the needs of the congregation, or to the desired impact of the sermons upon individual lives.

An explanation of three short-hand terms often heard when plans are being prepared may be useful: "needs," "means" and "ends." These are synonymous for three other terms typically used by planners: "need," "action" and "objective(s)," respectively. Translating the former into the latter may help.

> Needs: the situation/condition(s) to be changed, remedied or eliminated
>
> Means: the action required to produce the ends
>
> Ends: the new situation; result of action; product(s) or objective(s)

Giving proper attention to the distinction between the need and the desired result, or ends, will help significantly when designing a plan of action. Regardless of the terms used, results follow action.

So simple. So easily overlooked.

(The above explanation of needs, means and ends has been included here to help clarify how they could relate to the following chapters. However, for consistency and simplicity, generally, I have elected to use the more conventional terms, need, action and objective throughout.)

From Here to Reality

1. Is it worth the time that would be necessary for elders to help others in the congregation understand the distinction between the procedural steps of planning, and carrying out the plan? Why would this even be necessary? And if it is, who would benefit the most?

2. What are some common procedural mistakes that can be made when elders or others in a congregation begin to plan an activity?

— 8 —

Objectives Are Not Things You Do

Books in a box are not useful

Objectives are the results of the things you do. They are not actions or activities; they are outcomes or products. They are destinations. Achievements. Objectives should be stated as the final outcomes of a plan that will remain in existence after the plan has been completed.

Planners often confuse the objectives of a plan with the steps taken to produce them. Take a look at some existing congregational plans, a pastor's sabbatical leave proposal or any other request for financial support, whether it was successful or not, and you should find a section devoted to "Objectives." In many cases you will see that this section is simply a discussion, and often a rambling one, of what it is that someone or some group is going to do during the life of the plan. Then when you read the "Method," "Procedure," or "Implementation," section, you get more of the same. Many planners never define objectives clearly, though they think they do.

Stating objectives as planning or program outcomes has very important advantages. It will force the planning author or program director to clearly distinguish between what is to be *done* and what is to be *accomplished*. There is a way for a plan to present each with clarity and brevity. The relationships and distinctions between actions and objectives can be well-defined and obvious. As a result, those who read the proposed plan will be able to recognize the distinctions. This approach will force clear thinking and clarity of purpose.

I have served on proposal review committees where, after the proposed plans were read and discussed, reviewers still had great difficulty trying to distinguish between what would be done by program personnel, and what would be accomplished by the program. It was impossible to tell the difference between proposed input and projected output. Had objectives been stated explicitly as final products or outcomes, it would have been easy not to have missed the ultimate purpose of the plan.

Stating an objective as a product will also make it easier to prepare and implement a plan, and also to evaluate its eventual success or lack thereof. Once the proposed outcomes have been carefully stated, a method for determining the degree to which each has been achieved can be more easily designed.

If objectives are stated precisely and presented briefly in a simple list rather than in a narrative format, the proposed procedure for evaluating the degree to which each has been attained can be presented in a corresponding list relating each evaluative procedure to each objective. By presenting each in an easily compared manner, many pages of needless narrative will be avoided. This will make everyone happy, especially those who read the plan or proposal, those who will be asked to approve it, and ultimately those responsible for carrying it out.

A simple and straightforward way of writing objectives is to start with a statement similar to this: "Upon successful completion of this plan, the following objectives (or outcomes) will have been produced." This statement should be followed by a numbered list of objectives that will remain following cessation of the activities that produced them. If a plan will not produce lasting results, it shouldn't be proposed. If results cannot be predicted with some reasonable degree of definition and confidence at the time the plan is written, the plan should not be approved or even attempted.

Two illustrations will help to make the point. A church librarian requesting funds for new books might be tempted to state as an objective, "The purchase of three new copies of *Strong's Exhaustive Concordance of The Bible.*" Simply acquiring the books, no matter how necessary they may be, will be of no value if further action beyond their purchase and receipt does not occur. Consider this: the books, indeed, were purchased and received. This is exactly what the objective stated — the *purchase* of books. Nothing more. The stated objective was achieved. End of story.

But it shouldn't be. Books resting in a FedEx box was never the true objective.

In this situation, a more appropriately stated objective might be, "Three copies of Strong's Exhaustive Concordance of The Bible available for use by members of the Adult Doctrinal Study Class." This would get the box opened while assuring that the real reason for purchasing the books (the activity) had been accurately stated. This precision will create a relatively easy means of evaluating the success of the objective as well. Successful attaintment of this objective can then be proven by recording and reporting the number of hours the books are available for members of the class. Unless the books are actually available, they have no value, no purpose. Even though every librarian may understand this as one of the basics of the profession, the concept may easily be overlooked during the process of defining objectives and making the true case for funding the purchase.

A second illustration suggests how a pastor writing a proposal requesting funds for a study leave can apply the same method of stating objectives. Assume for this example that the pastor intends to prepare a monograph as one of several activities included in a larger plan. The preparation of the monograph is the activity; the actual manuscript will be the result—the objective. In this situation, the completed monograph will serve as proof that the objective was produced. Simple. Yet, during the same leave period the pastor may also engage in a two-week study tour in the Holy Land.

It would be easy to state that the study tour is the objective, but it may be a challenge to prove that study during the tour actually resulted in learning something—the true objective. This more specific focus will be helpful when attempting to prove that the tour produced the intended results. But, how to prove this? The answer need not be complicated. The simpler, the better. First, a proposed evaluation plan could include a commitment to submit photographic evidence or other validation that the tour took place. Anything that will prove that learning had actually occurred during the tour will be the most important component (e.g., copies of excerpts from a personal journal; a group-leader report of participant achievement; certificate of completion; or a publication or informal report resulting from the experience). Without oversimplifying the challenge, once the objective is stated as an end-result, a bit of creativity can usually provide the necessary proof. If a willingness to prove success is even attempted, it will go a long way to prove the sincerity and confidence of the planner. Regardless, it should be clear that a carefully stated objective is the key.

Objectives stated as outcomes will encourage those who control the approval process, and also those being asked to provide the necessary resources as an investment in the ultimate purpose. The potential for approval will be significantly enhanced if objectives are accompanied by a reasonable plan that will also provide proof of achievement.

In summary: When preparing any type of action plan, if you force yourself to state objectives as final products that will outlive the resources and activities that produced them, you will positively impress those being asked to approve the plan. You will even force yourself to be better able to clarify intent. Remember, objectives are not things you do, but the results of the things you do. Objectives are all that you have left after the work is done and the resources used to produce them are gone. They are your products; they must be predictable and provable.

From Here to Reality

1. Do you see anything wrong with stating objectives as things to be done within your congregation (such as holding prayer meetings, good preaching and home visitations)? If so, can you make a case for changing current practice? Or could there be an argument for making no change at all? If so, what would it be?

2. What difficulties may arise when encouraging others to view objectives as products? Do elders have a greater responsibility for understanding this concept than others? What steps could be taken to help congregational committees clarify and pursue their missions?

3. Is it more helpful to define an objective as a *product*, or a *result*? Can these terms be used interchangeably when applied to planning? Are there situations when one term might be more useful than another? If yes, what might they be? If no, why not?

— 9 —

Goal Versus Objectives

Not Synonyms

Definitions of the terms "goal" and "objective" vary with speaker and publication. Sometimes they are used synonymously, which makes little sense. It is fine to exchange the definitions between these two terms (as often found in the literature) as long as they remain the same throughout their use. For the purpose of understanding the following examples, and others found within these chapters, the terms are operationally defined below in a manner creating a clear distinction between each, and have been used throughout this book.

> Goal: A general statement of an anticipated outcome; more global in scope than an objective; not as easily proven to have been achieved given the nature of its longer-range projection; should be supported by at least one well-defined objective

> Objective: A specific statement of a projected achievement or product; states clearly what will remain after the activity that produced it has ceased; not a description of the activity; more easily observed in real-time than a goal; should be directly related to an existing need and subordinate to a desired goal; degree of achievement can be assessed by an evaluative procedure; can be strengthened by including reference to a specific timeframe and quantitative data

These definitions can be conveniently and easily used in real-life applications. The following goal and subordinate objectives applied to a congregation, will help illustrate this point.

Long-Range Goal

Pastors, elders and deacons who work together effectively and in harmony, achieving the goals and objectives of the congregational mission while fulfilling the mandate of the Great Commission.

Short-Range Objectives

Within two years of this date, the following will have been produced:

1. *An educational leadership program* encouraging and preparing future elders and deacons

2. *Two new elders*, each providing a unique contribution toward exercising careful spiritual oversight of the congregation

3. *Ten elder groups* within the congregation each consisting of no more than eight members for whom an elder will have oversight responsibilities

4. *A functional plan* in which elders and deacons work together in harmony, as they establish and conduct new mercy ministry, community outreach and Bible study programs within the congregation

5. *A carefully defined team ministry pastorate*, where the assignment of responsibilities to each of the pastors has been according to individual gifts and abilities and, in which synergistic productivity is maximized

Note that the projected achievement in each objective, italicized for emphasis, is not an action.

A sports analogy may be helpful. During a football game there are a number of sequential steps required before success can be claimed. Each requires careful planning and execution. Progress toward the goal (a score) is achieved by amassing success in consecutive short-range objectives (first downs). Downs, like objectives, must be successfully achieved before a goal can be realized. A score is dependent upon achieving the required number of first downs. A similar sequence of events is required in any planning effort.

If this analogy is taken a step or two further, it could be argued that winning the game is the mission and establishing a winning football legacy is the vision. I hesitate to compare coaches to elders, but the message should be clear.

To accomplish a mission, you must have at least one goal. To accomplish a goal, you must have at least one objective.

From Here to Reality

1. Do you think it is necessary for elders to insist that all members of a congregational planning committee understand the operational distinction between goals and objectives? What purpose would this serve? Should anything be done if some members resist taking the time to attend a pre-planning meeting where this technicality is clarified? If no, why not? If yes, suggest how this might be done.

2. Do you believe that the use of operational distinctions between goals and objectives raises any theological issues when planning spiritually-oriented events in the church? Explain.

3. Do you believe that stating spiritual objectives as specifically-defined and desired results, suggests minimizing the role of the Holy Spirit in planning? What about stating objectives only as general predictions, rather than as specific outcomes? What might be lost? What might be gained?

4. Are the distinctions between a goal and an objective as defined above compatible with, or in conflict with, those found in Scripture? (See ch. 3, The Scriptural Model.) What impact should this have on planning in the church?

— 10 —

An Inventory for the Future

A planning buffet

One of the most frequent but avoidable consequences of long-range planning is for the final plan to become lost to the corporate memory, and even to the memories of those responsible for its creation. Usually the state of being "lost" is more a function of the plan never having been recognized as being a practical component of the daily activities of the congregation. A form of mental relief can set in after many hours of planning, a convenient way of finally getting it out of the way, "at least for now." The intention, of course, is that the plan will be retrieved when it is needed. It is easy to assume that the plan is so fresh in minds, that it will not be forgotten. Yet, as is more often the case than anyone ever wants to admit, it will be forgotten—the fate of many a long-range plan. Beware of this memory trap; a failure of leadership!

Suggestion: Along with the congregation's mission statement, consider including a brief summary of the supporting long-range plan at the beginning of each elder and deacon meeting agenda. This may seem like sensory overkill or a waste of space, but it will keep the plan in front of those most responsible for its implementation. In like manner, it can also precede the printed agenda of each congregational meeting. This will assure that it will be available as a quick reference for every current and future decision.

Occasionally a long-range plan can be so comprehensive, that its length does not permit inclusion with an agenda or in any other easily manageable or summarized form that encourages frequent use. This leads to another suggestion: the creation of an inventory of short- and long-range objectives in the form of a document available for all future decision making. The document format should be such that items can be easily retrieved for ready and timely reference. Items appropriate to a particular meeting can be selected to appear with any agenda. An explanation is in order.

It is impossible to project most short-range plans with much accuracy beyond a three-year period, and most long-range plans usually beyond four or five years. When realistic planning is attempted beyond these limits, many of the longer-range objectives become not only more speculative, but possibly too numerous to be helpful in the short term. Thus, when a list of objectives becomes expansive (and there is nothing wrong with this if it is necessary and if it is done carefully), access and implementation can be accomplished more easily by using a unique approach—an "inventory for the future"—a single document. The short- and long-range goals and objectives included may extend well into the unpredictable future. This could lead to having the more futuristic objectives seen only as an amorphous wish list. Nothing is wrong with this if the inventory is clearly identified as just that; a list of desired expectations beyond those requiring near-term action.

The beauty of an inventory is that the items contained can be selected for action as circumstances require. Think "buffet table" loaded with objectives. Typically, a long-range plan is implemented according to an assigned sequential priority of objectives, often including a specific target date for the completion of each. This is a very useful and recommended planning technique. However, this is not as easily done when a plan requires an inventory approach that makes discretionary selection necessary over a longer period of time. The inclusion of target completion dates can still be very useful within a planning inventory, especially for the shorter-range objectives. Completion dates applied to much longer-range objectives, although less reliable, can be helpful as reminders of the need for necessary action at appropriate times.

An inventory format need not be complex. A simple list will suffice. It can be either arranged sequentially according to projected completion dates, or according to prioritized goals with supporting objectives appearing under each, or as a combination of these two approaches. Other variations can serve just as well, depending on the scope of the plan and the format most conducive to easy reference.

An example of a goal-ordered inventory of objectives follows. If desired, a date can be added parenthetically after each that proposes a time for completion. This is a useful option as it will serve as a target as well as a reminder.

An Inventory of Goals and Supporting Objectives

Goal: A thriving ministry within and outside the congregation (optional completion date)

> An adult Bible school program that addresses family issues (completion date)
>
> A comfortable, functional, well maintained and well managed nursery facility (completion date)
>
> A program developed by the deacons in which church facilities are available for community use (completion date)
>
> An on-campus lunch, fellowship and prayer group for local college students (completion date)

Goal: Elders equipped with the resources necessary to assure responsible shepherding within the congregation.

> Two new elders, each able to provide a unique contribution toward exercising careful spiritual oversight of members (completion date)
>
> An annual retreat program of ministry education for all elders and deacons (completion date)
>
> An allocation of pastoral assignments that assures the availability of time for meeting with individual members and adherents of the congregation (optional completion date)

This example could have been organized only as a list of objectives appearing sequentially according to their desired completion dates, rather than as objectives under specific goals as above. If this had been done, the dates would have served to put greater emphasis upon the passage of time, an often neglected component of long-range planning. This will require a way to show that each objective is related to a specific goal, if goals are referenced at all. A superscript, or numerical reference within parentheses following each objective (as used for a bibliographic reference), with a corresponding footnote, or endnote, related to the appropriate goal would suffice. Various format iterations are possible and are quite acceptable as long as the one used best serves the local needs and will allow easy reference.

An inventory, by its very nature, might continue for several pages. This is fine. Its purpose is to create a way of accommodating a lengthy list of planning objectives that extends well into the future, assuring that the objectives will not be lost to memory. Regardless of length or format, the concept remains.

From Here to Reality

1. What pitfalls and distractions could impede the useful application of an inventory of goals and objectives? Can these be avoided entirely? What precautions can be taken, and how and when might they be applied?

2. Which would be of more value: attempting to create and maintain a functional inventory, or simply revisiting and updating a more conventional set of short- and long-range objectives when the need arises? What problems might be encountered when using either approach?

— 11 —

Sensitivity to Gifts of Grace

Various gifts, the same Spirit

If the need for congregational planning is taken seriously by its elders, the time will arrive when it is necessary to determine who should assume responsibility for putting a plan together and making it work. An easy assumption is that it might be best to get an "outside expert" to direct the process. In many situations there may be wisdom in this, but not all congregations are alike in available resources, whether financial or experiential. Outside experts can cost money. For the benefit of congregations not inclined or able to access external planning help, a few words of caution as well as encouragement are appropriate when selecting a planning team from within the congregation.

First, a look at Scripture.

> *For as in one body we have many members, and the members do not all have the same function, so we, though many, are one body in Christ, and individually members one of another. Having gifts that differ according to the grace given to us, let us use them...* (Romans 12:4-6)

> *Now there are varieties of gifts, but the same Spirit; and there are varieties of service, but the same Lord; and there are varieties of activities, but it is the same God who empowers them all in everyone. To each is given the manifestation of the Spirit for the common good. For to one is given through the Spirit the utterance of wisdom, and to another the utterance of knowledge according to the same Spirit, to another faith by the same Spirit...All these are empowered by one and the same Spirit, who apportions to each one individually as he wills.* (I Corinthians 12:4-9, 11)

It is unmistakable. We are told that we must expect different people to have different abilities. This must be acknowledged. God made us this way for our common good. Elders must accept this biblical truth before beginning any serious planning, whether within the congregation or the broader denomination. To do otherwise is to neglect exercising a responsibility: The prudent use of existing gifts.

There is a tendency during the early stages of any kind of organizational planning to make certain that all stakeholders are represented. To do so is to encourage a lack of focus, even chaos; "too many cooks..."

Assembling a small energetic group of those having the most helpful gifts, rather than selecting those representing specific segments of the congregation, will assure fewer distractions, greater focus and more efficient progress. The concerns of unrepresented stakeholders should be addressed as progress reports are made to the elders and then incrementally to other essential groups (e.g., the deacons, finance committee, etc.) and ultimately to the wider congregation. The questions raised and suggestions received as the exposure to the plan is increased will provide opportunity for progressive refinement and further strengthening of the plan. I call this "progressive planning." The potential benefits of this approach will become obvious.

Now back to individual gifts. There may be those who desire to be a part of the initial planning group but who simply do not possess the necessary gifts, perhaps patience or vision. There may be others who are patient visionaries, but who do not desire to be part of the process. This is where it is important to recognize the need to exercise great sensitivity to both personal skills and desires, even encouraging those whose potential gifts have not been previously acknowledged within the work of the church. This is where an elder's personal acquaintance with individual members can be extremely helpful (a useful by-product of home visitation).

The gifts and motivations of some members may not be easily assessed. It should not be assumed that elders can determine whether a perceived call is from God or from self. Discretion is necessary. Remember that Noah must have been seen by his neighbors as a six-hundred-year-old kook, building something just as kooky in his backyard (Genesis 6 & 7). There is no reason to believe that he was previously known for his shipbuilding or sailing skills. But God called him anyway. There is no fail-safe formula for relating people, skills and responsibilities within the planning process. The most judicious approach may be to not assume the obvious and to not overlook the unobvious.

The point in all of this is that, basic to all planning efforts, the need to assign specific tasks to the most competent people available is essential. This applies to elders also. There is no reason to expect that elders have been innately gifted to deal with the idiosyncrasies and challenges of congregational planning just because they are elders. The previously expressed cautions for selecting members to participate in the planning process apply just as much to them.

Even though there is no proven prescription for how to select the best person for the job, great care in making the assignments is critical to success. This is a good place for prayer to permeate the process.

From Here to Reality

1. What are the risks an elder encounters when attempting to identify the best person for a particular assignment within the congregation? What are some good ways to avoid them? Can they be completely avoided? What experiences have you had that would be helpful to other elders as they approach this assignment?

2. Should an elder assume the responsibility of determining the differing gifts among members? Or would it be better to depend on a member's self-assessment?

3. An elder, as the chair of a committee, could easily be drawn into an uncomfortable situation when an obviously unqualified person insists on volunteering to help. Would it be wise for the elder to discuss I Corinthians 12 directly with the volunteer? Is it possible for an elder to be successful in such a situation? Or should providing this kind of help not be attempted? How would you counsel this elder?

4. Sequential exposure of a new plan to increasingly larger groups of people within a congregation is suggested. What is the reason for this? How many people should be involved at first? Should this number differ with the size of a congregation? How many can be too many? Can such a group be too small?

Planning with the Pastor

— 12 —

Compensation

First things first

I had considered omitting this topic entirely, but to have done so might have been interpreted as an oversight, or an unwillingness to address an elusive, sometimes difficult topic. Originally, I had decided that to include it might have been viewed as an insult to the reader. I could hear the reaction: "Of course appropriate and fair compensation for pastors should be a given." Indeed, an appropriate and fair salary must be a given! The need for a pastor's salary is not debatable, but what qualifies as "appropriate" and "fair" can be. This deserves careful attention. To be meaningful, each will need to be translated into quantitative reality.

First, appropriate. By appropriate, I mean compensation consistent with all employment criteria and existing and anticipated circumstances. I know of no pastor who has entered the profession for the money. I have been told of a pastor's wife who found it necessary to glean the discards of local grocery stores for her family's use. I once heard an elder insisting that a pastor should earn no more than members of the congregation, "because most of us are retired and on fixed incomes." True! Talk about impediments to a ministry! I suspect that as isolated as these incidents might appear, they could represent various unspoken financial challenges and frustrations other pastors and their families experience. Uncomfortable circumstances related to compensation should be anticipated, and they should be addressed before they happen. A vital ministry depends upon it.

Compensation must ensure that the pastor's focus remains on the congregation's mission, not upon food for the family or how to pay for some dental work. Appropriate compensation also should be an incentive for a pastor not to use income as reason for considering alternate employment, either in another congregation or another vocation.

There are numerous criteria upon which pastoral compensation could easily be based, some of which are not uncommon: a congregation's ability to provide; the pastor's previous experience; size of the pastor's family; how well the pastor preached the "interview" sermon; salary provided by the previous congregation; the average income of a congregation's members; the salaries of other pastors in the immediate community or throughout the same denomination; or a good guess by the elders as to how little the pastor will accept. Some of these can be helpful, others not. Even if several of these criteria were to be considered together, they would not necessarily provide a good formula for defining adequacy or fairness. The dilemma is obvious. There may be no perfect way, yet the need remains. This has to be faced every time a pastor is employed, and annual compensation is set. Every situation will be unique, thus defying a universal formula.

It is possible that the size of the pastor's family, or other personal obligations can become the overriding factors in establishing a compensation package, however, there is need to respect the basic conditions and purpose of the employer-employee relationship. That is, that compensation should be based primarily upon services rendered, as is the norm in other professional settings. This is not to say that consideration and compassion for the personal needs of the pastor should be ignored. Not at all. Yet, when a teacher is hired, compensation is based upon the teacher's qualifications and experience and the services expected by the school district, not the existing personal and family obligations of the teacher. Basically, there should be little difference between employing a teacher and employing a pastor. That being said, it is quite reasonable to acknowledge and respect the difference between a school district and a congregation. A school district is a corporation subject to public law and local policy. A congregation is a different creature, subject to its own policies and theology.

A congregation is the body of Christ (it is also likely to be incorporated in the state within which it resides). The Scripture tells us that in the body of Christ members should care for one another and that, "If one member suffers, all suffer together..." (I Corinthians 12:25-27). Although in some denominations the pastor may not be on the local roll as a member of the congregation per se, the pastor still must be considered a member of the body of Christ. This should be reason enough to assume the legitimacy of going beyond the typically accepted employment model, giving compassionate but reasonable attention to the pastor's personal needs when setting compensation. This will prevent "suffering" by both pastor and congregation. The short form of the story is that the pastor should be compensated commensurate with qualifications and experience, expected value to the congregation and with some *reasonable* and *measured* thought given to personal circumstances as may be appropriate.

I suggest that one of the minimal criteria should be compensation that permits the pastor to remain focused on the ministry and not upon personal and family needs. (My use of the word minimal neither proposes a norm nor suggests stinginess, but only a starting point.) This may not resolve the issue, but I propose it as a baseline from which to begin the process. Many factors will need to be considered, not just the ones that make up the base salary. "Appropriate" must also apply to fringe benefits. I encourage every congregation to base financial considerations on total compensation, not just base salary.

Then there is the issue of fairness. The assumption here is that fairness involves both parties, the pastor and the congregation. What may be fair to one may not be fair to the other. But it should be. The application of fairness, just as appropriateness, may require resolution through salary negotiation, an exercise to which leaders in ecclesiastical circles typically do not look forward. To avoid the challenges and likely discomfort of negotiating finances with a pastor, thoughtful preemptive action by the leadership will be required. This begins with the elders, or in some situations, with the deacons. In any event, both should be involved in some manner throughout the process. In many congregations, it may end with the entire congregation giving final approval.

There are any number of approaches to setting a pastor's annual compensation that will avoid the challenges of negotiation. Some may involve only the elders, only the deacons, both elders and deacons or their representatives, or possibly a committee. Some take the easy way out by depending only upon a previously agreed-upon formula. This may avoid the use of time and energies, but it also can be unnecessarily restrictive and uncaring, and eventually troublesome.

An excellent vehicle to use when facing the annual compensation challenge is the annual pastoral review. (See ch. 14, Accountability; Annual Review.) If the review is conducted near the end of the budget year, it can be held just before the annual congregational budget planning begins. This is an excellent time to discuss compensation directly with the pastor, in a mature, business-like, non-threatening manner. This will help avoid a take-it-or-leave-it approach to salary setting.

The simplest formula some use is to base compensation only upon a cost of living increase. A problem arises if the cost of living index falls, but pastoral performance improves, or remains the same. What then? The new annual increment compared to the previous year would be less, while the value of the pastor may have increased. Not exactly merit-based pay. A reduced cost of living adjustment actually can have the effect of a pay cut. I would not recommend a cost of living-only approach unless the cost of living index is supplemented by other factors such as merit or realigned responsibilities. That is, cost of living is a very legitimate factor to use, but it should not be the only one.

All this leads to a fine point of necessity: the need for a formal pastoral compensation philosophy, and a resulting operational policy. This is essential.

Without a standing philosophy of compensation, the approach to setting an annual compensation package has the potential for becoming inconsistent as inevitable changes occur in congregational leadership over time. A philosophy should not be left to individual or corporate memories. It need not be complex, possibly being as simple as the statement of a single goal followed by several appropriate objectives. The compensation policy need only include broadly-stated steps required to implement the philosophy each year. This will serve as a consistent annual guide to those responsible.

The specific steps used to arrive at the final compensation will depend upon the organizational makeup of the congregation and upon its leadership. Getting started may be difficult. The congregation must join the elders by first understanding the mission of the congregation and what resources it will take to achieve the mission. Providing for the pastor is the place to start.

In many congregations, the largest expense item in an annual budget is personnel compensation. It is also the most important. The pastor's total compensation must take priority over other expenses regardless of where the congregation is located along the somewhat predictable life cycle of a congregation. A new pastor is just as important to a young congregation as an experienced pastor is to a more mature congregation. Each is critical to the success of the ministry. And each must eat without the need for grocery store gleaning.

A congregation could be more willing to commit financial resources to a plan for improving the physical condition of the sanctuary than to do whatever is necessary with the same resources to attract and retain the pastor who would be most effective in the local ministry. The excitement of achieving a short-term objective that can be quickly realized and enjoyed can easily take precedence over one having the potential for the greatest impact over a longer period of time. Elders must enable a congregation to understand the wisdom of setting priorities in a meaningful way and how to go about it. This is leadership. This requires planning. It may also require patient but persistent "educational conversations" held informally with individuals, or more formally during a congregational meeting. Regardless of the venue, elders must take the initiative. Understanding the value of the pastor is essential to creating an attitude of willingness to provide appropriate and fair compensation. Dollars represent value, even in the church.

As inappropriate as it may appear to some, viewing a pastor as a commodity may help. A commodity is valued by its importance to the purchaser and consumer. How valuable is a highly qualified pastor to achieving a congregation's mission? Very! Value should not be based only upon what a pastor can and will be expected to do. Value is also a function of personal and professional qualifications that can be brought to the assignment. This includes educational preparation. Which leads back to the point that pastors are professionals. Compensation that reflects a professional calling is deserved.

Quantifying appropriateness and fairness will depend upon the two components of compensation: base salary and fringe benefits. A base salary can include a housing or equity allowance and can also take into consideration a number of other factors including cost of living increases and local real estate values if the pastor's residence is owned by the pastor. Fringe benefits can include health, life, and professional liability insurance, a retirement contribution, etc. Other required ministry expenses including local travel, hospitality, books and other publications, meeting and conference attendance, etc., should not be overlooked or confused with personal income. They should be included elsewhere in a congregation's budget, probably under "ministry expenses."

Determining and agreeing upon the real numbers to be put in the budget, and into which category they should be placed, can be a dreaded exercise not easily or comfortably faced. Much more could be said about the procedural steps that might be required, but my purpose here has been to draw attention to the fact that a pastor's compensation is not to be treated as being less important than the other matters of pastoral care.

It can't be stated too often: a pastor's compensation, at the very least, must be appropriate and it must be fair.

From Here to Reality

1. Why is agreeing upon a pastor's annual compensation often a difficult process? What can be done to make it easier, or to avoid difficulties all together?

2. What constitutes an appropriate and fair pastor's salary? Who should determine this, the elders or the deacons? Or both together? Is assigning this task to a compensation committee a good option?

3. Is your congregation's approach to setting the pastor's salary satisfactory to all involved? How could it be improved? What is the role of the elders? Should the congregation be involved? If so, how?

4. How might elders help a pastor who finds it difficult to live within an agreed-upon salary?

5. Is it proper to base a pastor's compensation upon factors beyond those commonly used to determine the compensation of other professionals (e.g., size of family, permanent health issues, etc.)? Explain.

6. Should the concept of merit-based compensation be applied when determining a pastor's salary? If not, why not? If yes, how and by whom should merit be determined? What procedural steps would be required if this concept were to be used in your congregation? Would it be worth the trouble?

7. Many believe that a pastor's salary should be the most important (not necessarily the largest) expense in a congregation's annual budget? How can those who may be unconvinced, be persuaded to agree with this priority? Are you persuaded? What should you do if you are one of only two elders who will defend this principle, while three other elders will not? What other budget items might compete for this budgeting priority?

— 13 —

Time Allocation

Tempus "fugits" for pastors too

Time is a gift of God. Its careless management can become a failing of the twenty-four-hour-seven-day-a-week pastor. The telephone must be answered regardless of the hour. Each meeting must be attended. Each sermon must be prepared. Each cry for help must receive a response. It never ends. The next thing the pastor knows, the week is gone, and over the years, so can be the pastor's health and conceivably the pastor's family. Also, the congregation!

The pastor's use of time, just as the passage of time, can be easily overlooked by the elders and not recognized as an elder responsibility. Double trouble! So, what are elders to do? The best place to start is to anticipate the problem. Plan ahead. Again, planning to the rescue!

One of the more difficult things for many people, including pastors, is to acknowledge the need for personal time away from all responsibilities, routine or not. This includes time for sleep, relaxation, exercise, family, reading and yes, even eating. My observations suggest that some pastors fall prey to these kinds of self-denial. Sometimes it might be deliberate. Sometimes the problem may not be recognized.

(Unfortunately, there may be the occasional pastor who needs encouragement to attend less to personal time and more to assigned responsibilities. Although this is not the focus here, the problem can be just as real and difficult to resolve. This also has to be addressed head-on by the elders if it becomes necessary.)

I have been acquainted with pastors who have always put others first, regardless of the day's schedule—even before their own families. I have known some, especially the ones who are new to their work, who strive to meet or exceed every elder-assigned and self-assigned expectation. Both types run the risk of personal neglect, be it physical, professional, marital or spiritual. This can lead to professional and even spiritual burnout. A pastor does not have to reach the time when the proverbial mid-career burnout happens, to be burned out. Elders must be alert to the causes. Also, to recognizing the symptoms.

A series of insightful observations may be necessary before elders recognize the problem. This can be difficult. Establishing a personal relationship, even a close friendship with a pastor will help. I believe an elder can be a good friend of a pastor without distorting the normally expected elder-pastor working and "authority" relationship. I will even go so far as to suggest that an elder should make every effort to become a good personal friend of the pastor. This requires discretion, but with care it can serve each well. It will facilitate the sharing of personal matters that could easily go unspoken, especially matters that may be contributing to pastoral stress.

Elders might consider taking a pastor to lunch. At first, this can be a once-in-a-while event, but over time may turn into something to be looked forward to on a more regular basis. There need not be a purpose other than to enjoy a meal together accompanied by some come-what-may conversation. I call this the "no-agenda lunch." The less casual the setting the better. The local pizza joint or hotdog shop will serve the purpose well; maybe even the picnic table in the churchyard. It can be amazing where such unpredictable moments might lead. Try it. It works.

As effective as the no-agenda lunch can be, human nature suggests that even when informal one-on-ones between friends take place, they can still involve uncomfortable moments. This is not reason to ignore the potential for personal friendship.

A more formal setting may be a better venue for some topics, such as time-use counsel. A pastor meeting with the elders during one of their regular meetings may not be the most comfortable venue, but it can have its advantages. Such topics need not wait for friendships to develop or problems to arise. They can be approached when employment begins. Better yet, time management should be a point of discussion and eventual agreement during pre-employment interviews.

Regardless of whether time-use conversations occur at the pre-employment stage or during mid-employment, they will provide opportunity for elders and pastor to establish a mutual understanding of purpose. This is far more helpful than waiting for the exit interview.

There are at least three general areas of importance: respect for the congregation's needs and ministry; respect for the pastor's personal welfare; and equal respect for pastoral responsibilities. Each must be addressed compassionately and directly. This is the time for conversation that establishes (or re-establishes) a no-nonsense understanding between elders and pastor.

Ideally, such conversations should be conducted in a business-like manner. It is best if they are focused on a written policy defining time-related criteria for both congregational responsibilities and the need for time away from the same responsibilities. The policy should be stated in a manner consistent with any other existing or developing employment arrangements with the pastor. Specific topics can vary, but six general areas of time-use are suggested: family and personal; congregation; study and renewal; vacations; sick days; and denominational service.

Below is an example of one way such a policy can be worded. It is not intended as a universally applicable policy, but simply a beginning point that invites modification to fit a local congregation and its needs. This example assumes more than one pastor in the congregation. It also suggests a rather generous allotment of personal time that will help create an environment conducive to pastoral vitality. Some may think it suggests too much personal time, but I have seen this generosity work to the advantage of both pastor and congregation over time. It can prove to be a wise investment.

If this contract-based example seems too officious, or the formality too uncomfortable, the same thing can be accomplished by a more informally written, guideline-type understanding between elders and pastor outside of a contract. Either way, it will serve the same purpose. Over time, all parties will recognize the wisdom of this contribution to pastoral vitality, and in turn, to a vital congregation.

The following example of a time-use agreement will provide a head start to elders as they help the pastor recognize the importance of personal time management. It will demonstrate that they have had the foresight to anticipate and plan for future problems, something a pastor may find surprising, even unexpected, and eventually something that will be greatly appreciated. This appreciation will become even more meaningful as pastor-elder-congregation relationships progress. The relationships will prosper better with it than without it.

Note that, for emphasis, family and personal time is referenced first. It can often be the most important and most difficult for a pastor to manage.

Signatures of agreement at the end may or may not be desirable. This a good place for the comfort factor to dictate.

Pastoral Time-Use Agreement

Family and Personal

We agree that one of the essential ingredients required to assure a vital pastor is the availability of time for family and self. We believe that achieving this may be difficult. Yet, we will work with you toward this end, encouraging and assuring that the following are found in your weekly schedule.

1. Regular and meaningful time set aside from pastoral responsibilities as "family time," that is, time available to be spent with your family in any manner desired; accountability to be reported in your regular monthly report

2. Sufficient time each week devoted to personal refreshment and edification, including appropriate exercise; accountability to be reported in your regular monthly report

3. Ideally, a five-day workweek, acknowledging that this will vary given the flexible circumstances typical of most salaried professionals.

4. Three personal days per calendar year. Days in excess of three will be considered vacation days; in extraordinary situations where this creates hardship, the elders may consider exceptions

5. Each full day away from regular pastoral responsibilities that is used for personal matters will be considered a personal day (e.g., for personal or family business, other family matters such as an illness, a death).

6. Occasional, non-routine use of brief periods of time for such personal matters as a medical appointment, trip to the bank, family errand, retrieving a child from school, etc., within a single work day will not be considered personal or vacation time.

7. Use of time that avoids the inclination "to take on too much"

Congregation

Given the typically unstructured nature of your weekly schedule, it can be difficult to predict and differentiate between time required by more general and routine activities (e.g., sermon preparation, study, personal devotions, meeting attendance, etc.) and the response time required by the occasional and unanticipated situation such as an urgent call for counseling during a member's personal crisis. We will make every effort to provide help with the following.

1. Assistance with regular responsibilities that cannot be carried out adequately due to temporary and/or permanent interruptions requiring redirection of attention and effort.

2. Managing unexpected and potentially stressful matters.

Study and Renewal

All too typically, there is little or no opportunity available to take a meaningful "break from it all" in order to engage in some much needed relaxation, or time for extensive study. It is also acknowledged that time to accommodate a meaningful leave must be assured before planning for the leave can begin. Thus, as elders, we are committed to assure that the availability of periodic leave time will always be a permanent priority, an integral part of time allocation.

Accordingly, we pledge a firm commitment to make meaningful periods of time available that are dedicated to further professional development and personal refreshment in the form of a Pastoral Study and Renewal

Leave. This may also be treated as a sabbatical leave. Such a leave will be based upon the following criteria.

1. Following each sixth year of service, a six-month Pastoral Study and Renewal Leave at full compensation, or a twelve-month leave at half the annual compensation, at your discretion, will be available. Full fringe benefits will be provided regardless of which option is selected.

2. Eligibility for the same amount of leave-time will follow each subsequent six-year period of full-time service or its equivalent.

3. The Pastoral Study and Renewal Leave can be available in smaller whole-month increments during the same year, if and as you may desire, and as approved by the elders.

4. The intended spirit of this option is to provide meaningful opportunity for either an extended time of study and/or renewal, or shorter periods available as may be required by unique opportunities and circumstances. It is not intended to be used for occasional personal travel, multiple or long weekends, combination with existing vacation time, or purposes other than significant longer-term investments of time directly related to study, personal renewal or the local ministry.

5. Regardless of the length of leave-time increments used within the leave period, unused leave-time may not be used beyond the same leave-year or applied to a future leave period. That is, leave-time may not be "banked."

6. Compensation will be prorated in an equitable manner consistent with the length of the leave and as determined by the elders and deacons, and arranged with the treasurer.

7. Use of leave-time will assume agreement and obligation to return to regular full-time responsibilities for a period equal to a minimum of two years per one-year leave, with shorter commitments to be prorated at an equivalent rate. Failure to comply will require the return of all congregational compensation provided during the leave plus other related financial obligations assumed by the congregation (e.g., pulpit supply) that might have been required.

8. The manner in which the leave is used is to be self-determined. It is to be proposed in a written plan to be approved by the elders, describing how the leave will contribute to your personal needs, and to the enhancement of the congregation's ministry.

9. If pastoral performance issues should warrant, or in the event of any misuse of approved leave-time as determined by the elders, the elders retain the right and responsibility to modify the conditions and availability of future pastoral leaves.

10. Time and related expenses will be provided for attending at least one ministry-related conference per calendar year at your discretion (beyond normal attendance at denominational conferences and meetings required by a denominational committee assignment or other responsibility).

11. Encouragement will be provided toward the pursuit of continuing academic study, including advanced degree-related opportunities. Assistance will be provided to the extent possible, including possible financial support and help with necessary arrangements, as resources may be available at the time.

12. An annual allowance, to be determined with the elders, will be available for the purchase of books and other resources related to the local ministry; payment method(s) to be arranged with the Treasurer.

Vacation

1. "Vacation" is defined as time away from pastoral responsibilities, normally in increments of 24-hour days.

2. "Vacation" does not include regular absences for attendance on behalf of the congregation at denominational meetings; regular annual local, regional and other denominational conferences where significant program responsibilities, such as being a speaker, have been assigned; and occasional committee or other meetings and retreats related to denominational responsibilities. This will assume that only one denominational family conference involving responsibilities is attended in the same budget year.

3. Normally accepted major national holidays (i.e., Thanksgiving, Christmas, New Year's Day, Memorial Day, Independence Day and Labor Day) should not be treated as vacation days, but as "days off" with no reduction in compensation.

4. Three weeks of vacation time per 12-month period during the first three years of employment will be available, increasing to four weeks in the fourth and following years.

5. A "week" is defined as a period of seven consecutive days that includes one regular preaching day.

6. Maintaining a personal vacation record, and sharing it periodically with the elders is your responsibility.

7. Normally, vacations should be taken in traditional whole-week increments ranging from one to four weeks in duration.

8. Two "vacation weeks" per 12-month congregational budget-period may be "banked" for use in the following 12-month period. Banked weeks may only be used during the year immediately following the year in which they were earned.

9. Each vacation period is to be arranged with and approved by the elders.

10. Each vacation request is to be submitted at the time of the annual elder planning meeting, but no later than January 31 of the calendar year during which the vacation is proposed. Requests submitted at other times will be considered only on a "first-come, first-served" basis, with approval being tempered by existing circumstances.

11. Vacation requests will be reviewed and approved with the welfare of the congregation being a high priority.

12. Vacation time approval will be coordinated with the other pastor(s).

13. If vacation requests of more than one pastor are received for the same period of time, and unless extraordinary circumstances should dictate otherwise, priority will be given to the first request received, and/or the earliest date of original employment. Normally, concurrent vacation time for both pastors will not be approved.

Sick Days

1. Normally, seven "work" days may be used annually as sick days with no change in compensation. Extraordinary situations involving extended illness (e.g., sick leave) will be handled on a case-by-case basis, and could involve a reduction in compensation.

2. A "work day" is defined as one day of regular weekly preaching plus any day, Monday through Saturday, per seven-day period, excluding vacation days and your regular weekly "day off."

3. Sick days may not be banked, and are to be used only in the calendar year in which they become available.

Denominational Service

1. We will normally honor, and even encourage your positive response to a legitimate request for help that may come from another congregation, committee, board, or other need of the denomination, or from other ministry-related organizations or associations. Normally, such involvement outside the congregation will not be considered as vacation, or personal days, but will be viewed as an extension of the congregation's ministry.

2. No-cost pulpit exchanges with other congregations are encouraged when a clear benefit to at least one of the congregations is evident. When possible, we are to be advised well in advance of the date of the proposed obligation, and prior to acceptance of the commitment. Normally, approval will be forthcoming if the pulpit can be filled and other pastoral responsibilities assumed by another pastor of the congregation, or other reasonable arrangements can be made.

3. Only in unusual circumstances will approval be given for an absence requiring preaching by a pastor not regularly employed by the congregation.

4. In all situations, congregational priorities must be assured.

Attention to these topics will reduce and even eliminate anxiety that can be caused by unanticipated events. It will increase the pastor's ability to concentrate on ministry objectives, while having complete confidence in how the elders will respond to time adjustments required by future events. This will be a win-win for pastor and elder. Also, a win for the congregation. Elders can be kept abreast of how time has been spent by means of the pastor's monthly activity report to the elders (See ch. 14, Accountability).

It may be advisable to be more specific in some of these areas than what this format suggests, establishing the hours or days recommended or required for each activity. This could help in allocating time for family, and restricting time for extra-congregational commitments. Discretion must be used here, as overregulation of time can treat the pastor more like an hourly employee, than a professional. Not good.

A reminder: there are occasionally time-related issues that come close to defying solution. When a pastor uses Monday as a regular weekly "day off," and Monday turns out to be a holiday, as for example, Labor Day, what then? Does the pastor lose a day off? Or should Tuesday become the default day off for that week? Even if both Monday and Tuesday are assumed to be available for the pastor's personal use, the pastor's work load for the same week is not reduced proportionally. It may also escape the elder that national holidays are often good opportunities for church picnics. Not only is the pastor expected to show up for the picnic, but it will require spending more time with the very people from whom the pastor needs a day away. How does the pastor enjoy a Thanksgiving holiday when an additional sermon must be prepared for delivery at the community Thanksgiving service?

These kinds of circumstantial anomalies cannot always be easily incorporated into a time-use policy. Yet, it can be assumed that they will occur from time to time. Rather than attempting to write a policy that anticipates every possible eventuality, the most important thing is for elders to be alert to this, and to respect the pastor's personal time, recognizing that circumstances change. Good, open communication will help immensely. So will compassion and flexibility.

Another reminder: time costs money. This generally accepted truism applies to the church just as it does elsewhere. How this applies to a congregation may not be immediately obvious or understood, especially in some situations. An example might be when a pastor is seen attending a parent-student "play day" and picnic at the school with a son, or on the local golf course with a daughter. The costs of these activities to the congregation could be described as "unseen costs"—very real, but not very obvious. They are very real because they are included within the compensated time allocation under the category of "Family and Personal." This congregational expense will not be as obvious as other time-related costs, as for example, when a pastor is preparing a sermon or counseling a teen. In the golf course example, some may not see the pastor as attending to assigned responsibilities per se. This kind of time-use might appear as compensation for time "not on the job." The flexible use of time should be remembered by the elders as having been encouraged within the parameters of the time-use agreement. Any member inquiring about the school picnic or the golf course sightings should be advised accordingly.

Pastoring is a twenty-four-hour-a-day responsibility. It is not a collection of on-and-off-off-the-clock individually accountable responsibilities. A pastor is not paid by the hour. Compensation is composed of a salary and fringe benefits as is true for most other professionals. And a professional's day is usually different from the next day, or from the previous day. Thus, each day can involve activities that generate compensated costs for a variety of very acceptable activities. Pastoral accountability, therefore, must be based upon total performance, not upon a series of directly chargeable activities.

Calling attention to the distinction between the types of legitimate employment costs may sound like creating concern for a problem that does not exist. Almost true. But a misunderstanding of the relationship between personal time and ministry time has the potential for creating unnecessary tension between elders and deacons, and even within the congregation. Elders should work toward avoiding this kind of problem before it arises. This is a place where careful planning and good elder-deacon communication is required (See ch. 19, "Team Leadership").

When a pastor's employment agreement is being prepared, cooperation between elders and deacons will help. This is good reason for involving deacons in the early stages. In a similar manner, keeping the congregation informed and even involved as appropriate will prove to be extremely valuable. It will help all to understand that the elders have determined that the pastor is to be viewed and treated as a professional, rather than as a closely monitored hourly employee. This is good planning. It is also good "eldership."

> *"Time is a resource that is nonrenewable and nontransferable. You cannot store it up, slow it up, hold it up, divide it up or give it up. You can't hoard it up or save it for a rainy day—when it's lost, it's unrecoverable. When you kill time, remember that it has no resurrection."*
>
> David Baker, in "Jazz Man," Indiana Alumni Magazine, November–December 2010; page 28

From Here to Reality

1. When considering the importance of every day and every moment, is it proper to refer to time as God's gift, God's other gift, or simply as a gift from God? Are there distinctions? Does it matter?

2. What are some examples of how a pastor's time can be misused? Are some examples less important than others, or is all misuse misuse, regardless of degree? Does pastoral misuse of time require preemption or intervention?

3. How can an elder evaluate how a pastor uses time when the elder is unlikely to be able to make the necessary personal observations?

4. Does your pastor ever appear to be misusing time? If yes, how would you, as a concerned elder, recommend that the matter be addressed? If no, should you suggest that the pastor be rewarded in some manner? How? Would a reward be appropriate, or should the efficient use of time be a normal expectation?

5. Has it been possible for your pastor to take one day off each week? What circumstances can make this difficult? Have they been experienced by your pastor? On a day off, should your pastor be

encouraged to "take the phone off the hook?" If this is not done, is it really a day off? What are the options?

6. How much say should one pastor have over the other pastor's use of time spent on shared responsibilities within a two-pastor pastorate? What are the issues? How, and by whom should conflicts be resolved? How could they be avoided?

7. Would a Pastoral Time Agreement as proposed in this chapter work in your congregation? What modifications would help make the agreement more applicable to your local circumstances?

8. How can a pastor who refuses to take a much needed leave, be required to do so without destroying what is otherwise a very congenial elder-pastor relationship? What should be done if refusal continues? Which is more important, keeping peace by taking no further action, or doing something because the congregation's ministry is so dependent on the vitality of its pastor?

9. How are your pastors' daily schedules different from those of other professionals? How are they similar? What problems might you encounter when helping your pastor avoid being overwhelmed by being "on call" at any hour of the day or night? Are creative solutions possible, or is this just the way a pastor's life has to be?

10. Would it be fair to use a physician's work week as a standard against which a pastor's work week is compared? Are expectations versus performance the same, or just similar? Is there a better way to help one understand the potentially intense schedule of a pastor?

11. How can a no-agenda-lunch be of value to both pastor and elder? Should arranging this be a formally assigned elder responsibility, or should this relationship just develop naturally? How many elders should be involved at a time? Can the no-agenda-lunch become too routine, or should it be just a when-time-permits event?

12. Does Professor David Baker offer something of value to the church?

— 14 —

Accountability

Big help, not big brother

The elder is to be responsible for the spiritual welfare of the congregation. This is a responsibility of compassion and love for every individual. It should not be missed that the pastor is also a member of "the flock," also requiring and deserving the elders' very careful oversight. Because of the pastor's unique role within the congregation, attention must also be directed to issues beyond the pastor's spiritual welfare and ministry per se. This will require the investment of elder time on things that may otherwise be easily viewed as being too mundane, unimportant or even unnecessary.

Opportunity for accountability must be a major component of the help pastors receive; specifically, accountability to their elders, and thus to the congregation. I have sensed that good pastors appreciate being held accountable. Accountability must not to be interpreted as a call for elders to always be "keeping an eye on" their pastors, and certainly not to micromanage their daily schedules. Not at all. It is a call to assist the pastor. It is a call for elders to help protect the pastor's daily schedule from inefficiencies, so it can contribute most effectively toward a vital pastor. The focus here is on two suggestions that will help pastors maintain an appropriate balance among their varied and often stressful responsibilities; a monthly report and an annual review.

But first, a word of caution. There can be a very fine line between friendship and "eldership." In many ways, there need not be a line at all. There is no reason elders and pastors cannot be good friends. As I have emphasized previously, I believe that an elder must have great compassion and concern for the pastor as a "person," that is, as a living, breathing human being having the same needs and emotions we all have.

This can and should lead to a personal friendship that extends beyond the more formal elder-pastor relationship normally expected and observed within the church. As in any relationship where one person is responsible for the oversight of the other (in this case, the elder for the pastor), there is always danger that the friendship will intrude in an unhelpful manner upon the responsibility. Human nature is fraught with weaknesses, one of which can be to let an affection, even a "professional affection," for another person override good and fair judgment.

I can say from experience that it is difficult to carry out corrective measures involving a person over whom one has authority, especially when that person is a trusted colleague who has become a good friend. Consider how hard it would be to reprimand, or even fire a close, faithful associate of long standing. Therein lies the problem. How can an elder establish a personal working relationship and friendship with a pastor, while at the same time maintaining a proper authority relationship within the church? This can be answered in various ways, many of which will be dependent upon the personalities, maturity, experience and interpersonal skills of both elder and pastor.

An awareness of, and respect for the potential problems that can arise are essential. This is where the elder must take the lead by example. The authority-friendship relationship is best initiated, and most easily controlled by the elder. This may be one of the most important factors in establishing a good working relationship between elders and pastor. It need not be based upon rules, guidelines and other such formalities. It needs to be based upon good judgment.

I have included this topic here as I believe much can be accomplished toward diffusing the potential tensions between authority and friendship. Toward this end, I recommend the use of the monthly pastor activity report and annual review. Conversations made possible by these regularly scheduled and anticipated reviews will be helpful in maintaining the necessary balance. They will provide opportunity for the professional friendship to develop naturally within the framework of an authority relationship.

Monthly Activity Reports

It is very easy to let time pass without ever inquiring about how the pastor is proceeding with normally expected responsibilities, let alone the myriad of other unexpected urgencies that always find ways to intrude into a daily schedule. The pastor may not be inclined to report the many smaller but often stress-producing intrusions. This is too bad and can be avoided. Help is as close as the caring elder. Or it should be.

A simple first step is for the elders to request a monthly report, summarizing the pastor's activities of the most recent calendar month. Ideally, this should be distributed to the elders one week in advance of the regular elder meeting. Yes, this too will consume a bit more of the pastor's time. But if the report is viewed as an instrument of mutual trust and purpose, the cost of the time invested in its preparation and review will soon be recognized as a distinct benefit to both the pastor and elder. It can create many opportunities not otherwise possible.

The use of a carefully thought-out report format can serve as an encouragement to include such things as interactions with specific individuals during the month. It will draw attention to the amount of personal shepherding in which the pastor has engaged, and with whom the shepherding has taken place. The number of member contacts may be important, but even more important may be the names of individuals that may reappear in the report more frequently than others over time. The alert elder will see this as an opportunity to inquire about the individual, while drawing the attention of other elders to a possible need of which they may not be aware. Other situations will also become more obvious, suggesting opportunities where elders can volunteer to help their pastor. These can include, for example, certain home visits or unpleasant confrontations between individuals in the congregation where help is required to diffuse difficult interpersonal issues.

Three things will be accomplished: greater awareness by the pastor of how personal time has been consumed; increased awareness by the elders of how the pastor's time is being allocated to various parts of the ministry; and possibly even more importantly, an awareness of less obvious circumstances within the congregation where elders should be involved.

Concern for maintaining good communication between elder and pastor is not typically a topic receiving much, if any, attention. Over time, the lack of frequent contacts with the pastor can create an "uncomfortable distance." Occasional conversation is an easy way of sharing in the ministry by staying in touch. It need not be formal. It can take place over the no-agenda-lunch, while sharing a ride to a meeting or during a seventh inning stretch. Informality will lend itself to spontaneity, and spontaneity to familiarity. As good as this sounds, it still can be difficult to achieve. Busy schedules interfere; another reason for an activity report.

The activity report also can be very helpful in dealing with an uncomfortable situation. This could be when a pastor is not fulfilling responsibilities in an effective manner. The cause might be attributable to a lack of time-use discipline, an inability to recognize cause and effect relationships, preoccupation with personal family matters or any number of other reasons. Regardless of the reasons, and acknowledging the potential awkwardness of remedial conversations with the pastor, elders will have a unique opportunity. The monthly report presents a periodic, "comfortably available" time for helpful conversation that need not by itself generate confrontation. This is not unlike having a standing topic on any committee or board agenda automatically providing opportunity to review a topic without requiring it to have been brought up by one individual. It will reduce the possibility that an individual (in this case, an elder) might be blamed for raising the topic and creating what could appear to be a more personal matter than it really is. This new "compassion factor" will introduce an unobtrusive way of contributing to positive pastor-elder relations—even friendships.

The monthly report should not be unnecessarily time-consuming for either the pastor or the elders. A few basic reporting categories can serve as a guide to the pastor without limiting reporting creativity, or requiring an inordinate amount of time to prepare. Of course, the expectation is that the pastor will be forthright and appropriately inclusive in record keeping.

A simple reporting format that has proven very successful follows. This is not intended to be prescriptive, only suggestive. Variations should be considered that will more directly accommodate local needs. Reporting categories should be required only when they will produce data not otherwise available, and only data that will be helpful to both pastor and elders. Not to be overlooked is the report's usefulness for providing not only evidence of time-use inefficiencies and uncovering special needs, but also identifying areas where additional pastor support (e.g., electronics, staffing, etc.) may be needed.

Activity Report

Inclusive Dates (reporting period)

Personal Time (family, exercise, etc.)

Sermon Preparation (preparation time in hours)

Preaching (sermon topics, venues, etc.)

Teaching (Bible school classes, small groups, etc.)

Individual Shepherding (names; not issues)

Hospitality (individual, group, etc.)

Evangelism (outreach/community involvement, etc.)

Denomination (regional, national; committee work, conference calls, etc.)

Other (whatever may be helpful)

There is a trap. If not carefully monitored, this report can become burdensome, a defeat of purpose. It must not be allowed to become a daily diary or a moment-by-moment, hour-by-hour record of every activity such as each phone call or description of how study-time was spent. There is also the danger of the focus becoming job performance rather than ministry effectiveness. Generally, job performance should be addressed annually, not monthly. The pastor must be counseled to view the monthly report as an opportunity, not an inquisition.

Annual Review

There is a second reporting mechanism that also can be as helpful to the pastor as to the elders: the annual review. This is a vehicle used in other professions, sometimes called a performance review. There is a danger here. Misuse can lead the pastor to become obsessed with the notion that this also can be more of an inquisition rather than an opportunity. The possibility always exists that an inordinate amount of time throughout the year will become focused on preparing for the review, rather than on carrying out the duties to be reviewed. I have observed this in other than a church setting where misdirection of energies resulted in poor performance, and ultimately job termination, the exact opposite of what was intended. With care, this can be avoided. One way is for the elders to insist that the review be focused first upon the pastor's personal and professional well-being, followed by personal performance and ministry objectives. This will require careful thought, but it can be done.

I am not suggesting that performance is of less importance. Without proper attention to "the personal," the pastor's performance can never be as effective as it should be. Just as with the monthly report, a mutual understanding of purpose well in advance of the review will accomplish two very important things. It will establish that the review is an opportunity for the pastor to share personal and ministry realities within a positive environment. The review also will be a way for the elders to assess areas where they can be of greater help to the pastor, thus ultimately to the congregation.

Again, a rather simple and straightforward format that has proven successful for focusing discussion during the review can accomplish both purposes. It will neither assume nor require a written pastor's report, thus encouraging a low-key conversational approach. (If a permanent written record would be helpful, this can be required, but I suggest that it be avoided.) This format is based upon what an educator might call "thought questions," what a politician might call "talking points"; topics that should generate considerable pre-meeting thought, and thus a reduction of unnecessary and unanticipated conversational tension and surprises during the review. To assure success, the agreed-upon format should be made available well in advance of the conversation, preferably even a year earlier. Further, sufficient time for good discussion should be allowed for the meeting; at least an hour, possibly two.

Annual Review

The purpose of the annual review is to provide opportunity for you to review your recent year's activities with the elders, with attention given to how personal matters (family, finances, time-use, available resources, need for change, etc.) may be impacting your ministry. This will be a verbal review (conversational, not written) to assure that together we are providing for our congregation's spiritual growth in the best possible ways. The following topics will serve as a general outline for our conversation. Topical explanations are intended only as guidelines and suggestions for thought. Opportunity will be available to discuss additional topics.

Family: time with family; specific needs of spouse and children; ways elders can help; other

Personal: health, physical fitness, stress; time management; satisfaction; disappointments; professional development needs; finances; ways elders can help; other

Year In Review: general overview of activities; objectives met or not met; time allocation; program efficiencies; successes; failures; satisfaction; disappointments; congregational strengths and weaknesses; suggestions for change; new programs; refinement or elimination of programs; ways elders can help; other

Ministry/Congregation: observations and comment; spiritual matters; congregational oversight; mission, goals and objectives; time allocation; suggestions for change; support resources; satisfaction; ways elders can help; other

Denomination: impact on time required for congregational responsibilities; contributions made versus time invested; satisfaction; disappointments; ways elders can help; other

Community: specific activities; time required; contributions made versus time invested; relation to congregational mission; value to community versus value to congregation; satisfaction; disappointments; ways elders can help; other

Year Ahead: new personal objectives; suggestions related to congregational mission and ministry; recommendations for change; ways elders can help; other

Additional Topics: anything you would like to discuss

Note that following each topic is a suggestion that the pastor advise the elders as to how they can be more helpful. I believe this to be of sufficient importance that if the pastor does not respond to this prompt, then the elders should raise the topic. This will reinforce the notion that the pastor is not alone in the ministry.

By requiring nothing in writing, the emphasis will be upon the purpose of the report, not upon the formality, personal challenge and the physical appearance of a written narrative. This will make better use of the pastor's time and direct focus to what is important, proving to be another win-win-win for the pastor, the elders, and the congregation.

From Here to Reality

1. Have your elders ever experienced difficulty establishing a workable accountability relationship with your pastor on matters of performance? Have they ever discussed this with your pastor? What types of interpersonal friction have been experienced, or might be expected? How can this be managed effectively, yet amicably?

2. Can requiring a monthly pastor's report to the elders create more trouble than it is worth? How can it be determined if a report is a good fit for your elder-pastor relationship, and for the good of the congregation? Should the pastor have to agree to a monthly report before it is required?

3. What should be the highest priority topic included in a pastor's annual review? Should this be determined by the pastor, or by the elders? Should it remain the same each year, or be changed according to circumstances?

4. In your situation, would a written pastor's annual review be of more value than one conducted verbally? Would there be any merit in a report that is part written and part verbal? What other alternatives exist and under what circumstances might they be used?

5. Is requiring a monthly activity report and an annual review compatible with the view that a pastor is a professional? Or that the pastoral ministry is a calling?

— 15 —

Let the Pastor Be Pastor

Getting what you pay for

The assignment of a pastor's ministry responsibilities must take into account the resources that allow the time necessary to perform them well. Regardless of a congregation's means, pastors who are required to do their own clerical chores are being overpaid for assuming such responsibilities. Easily overlooked is that pastors are often expected to do things such as prepare the weekly printed worship program, prepare and send routine correspondence, respond to casual but important telephone, postal and email inquiries and be involved in the time consuming preparation of the facility prior to a meeting. Money paying for the time intended for pastoral responsibilities, but diverted to time for clerical and administrative tasks or custodial services, is money being spent unwisely. It is also an inefficient use, actually a misuse, of a pastor.

Time spent on clerical and/or administrative matters cannot possibly be spent at the bedside of an ailing member. The reality that one cannot be two places at the same time, applies well here. This is an either-or situation; either pastors are doing what they have been called to do, or they are doing someone else's job. Elders must be careful to protect the pastor from these subtle but very real time consuming intrusions, however important they may be. There are ways to do this.

Especially for the smaller congregation, this can be a legitimate problem. Nevertheless, this has to be given serious consideration if pastors' energies are to remain focused on ministry matters, and not on energy-draining distractions. This should be addressed clearly at the time of the pastoral call and within the final employment agreement. It also needs to be addressed within a congregation's annual budget. The necessities referenced below are considered minimal and normal for most pastorates. Others will develop naturally as the ministry grows, the need increases and experience is gained.

Baseline necessities that should be included when planning for pastoral support include the following. A two-pastor team ministry is assumed.

1. A buffer (i.e., a person) between the pastors and those desiring access to them
2. Time-management assistance (e.g., help maintaining and coordinating calendars, meetings, etc.)
3. Communication assistance (email, phone calls, unexpected "drop-ins," etc.)
4. Occasional representation of pastors in their absences (e.g., at meetings, events, etc.) as may be necessary and appropriate (elders can help here)
5. Computer and other basic office-type and personal electronic support devices (e.g., internet access, printer and copier, cell phone, etc.)
6. Good work space and meeting space, seating, lighting, shelf space, etc.
7. Assistance with occasional incidental responsibilities (e.g., making meeting and travel arrangements, contacting individuals, purchasing supplies, record keeping, etc.)
8. Qualified clerical/administrative personnel for the responsibilities above

Arranging for these support services raises several important issues and questions. For example: full- versus part-time help; if part-time, how many hours per day and week; proper staff compensation; recruitment of the most qualified (not necessarily the most available) person; available space; total cost of services including staffing, equipment and supplies; and the availability of funding required.

As time passes, the ratio of clerical versus administrative support will likely change in the direction of the administrative. There may be a temptation to compensate persons at an administrative salary level when they are expected only to perform hourly clerical duties. This is an easy mistake to make, especially when a highly qualified member of the congregation may agree to serve in a lesser role. Compensation should be consistent with services provided, and not at the level of one having credentials beyond those required by the position. Emotions and personal relationships must not override good judgment.

Of note is that in recent years the term "administrative" has been increasingly applied to responsibilities that have been traditionally considered clerical. I believe this has been done to make clerical duties appear to be more sophisticated than they may actually be, thus attracting a greater applicant pool. I have found that a position-title upgrade may be more important to an employee than increased compensation, even for an incumbent. There was a day when "administrative" (as in administrative assistant) was applied to duties more directly associated with those of a superior who the assistant was supporting (e.g., making occasional management decisions, discretional scheduling, "standing in" at off-site events, etc.). But no longer. Things have changed. I am proposing nothing more than being aware of this generational change in employment terminology when arranging for support staff. The operational distinction between administrative and clerical should remain a local option. I have no recommendation, except to be aware of what these terms may mean to others.

In some circumstances, especially in the smaller congregation, when space availability is an issue a remote location could be considered for support personnel. Given today's electronics, new and creative communication options are available. The physical locations of the support person and the pastor need not always be the same.

Even for the pastor, an office location other than in the church building might be an attractive possibility. Experience suggests that an off-site office (*e.g.* the pastor's residence) can work just fine. This could provide greater efficiencies, especially in the use of time. A home office can help protect study and sermon preparation time from "interruption time." With proper arrangements, telephone calls can be taken by a staff person at another location. Yet, it takes little imagination to recognize that the home office is not immune to interruption, especially family interruptions. This simply requires a decision as to which venue will provide the greatest efficiencies.

If a support person could work from home, it might be possible to attract a candidate who might not otherwise be available. It would also free up space in the church building that could then be dedicated to another purpose (e.g., conferencing, counseling, teaching, etc.). If different locations were to be used by a support person and by the pastor, some redundancy of equipment would be necessary, an additional expense. It is possible that this cost could prove to be a "wash," or even a net saving when all things are considered. Another possible downside is that there would not be a person in the church building on a regular basis during the day. This could affect building security and make it more difficult for someone desiring to locate a pastor. A solution might be a part-time staff person on site during predictable office hours, another additional cost. Careful analysis could show how some combination of on and off-site locations could actually become of value when considering such things as utility costs, travel time, avoidance of unexpected interruptions and space savings.

The pastors should be asked to submit an assessment of the predicted clerical and/or administrative assistance needed by each, and an estimate of support hours likely to be required. Predicting the hours could be difficult. A reasonable estimate might be that between twelve and twenty hours per week could suffice, at least at first. Within this range, hours can be configured in any number of options, including, for example, three or four 3-hour days; four or five half-days; or three, approximately six or seven-hour days per week. At the outset, hours and exact time periods should remain flexible.

It is wise that when the decision is made, a predictable daily and weekly schedule be part of the plan. This will ensure a consistent pattern for the benefit of support staff, and for anyone desiring to access a church representative. This also will be very helpful to pastors as they budget their use of time. The pastors should be given considerable say in whatever scheduling arrangements are made, even to the point of being entirely responsible for the decisions. Schedules must remain flexible, anticipating unexpected events and the need for modification as time passes.

From Here to Reality

1. What if your pastor does not want any clerical help? Can this present a problem? If yes, how might the problem become a larger problem, or even lead to additional problems? Are your elders best equipped to resolve the matter, or should this matter be referred to the deacons?

2. Do you think a buffer between your pastor and others during office hours and times of study would improve your pastor's efficiencies? What kind of buffer would work best in your church: a sign on the door, a notice in the weekly worship program stating office hours or a receptionist? Is it wise to tell the congregation that "the door is always open?" Which method would be best for preserving a wholesome pastor-member relationship in your congregation?

3. The use of multiple locations to support the pastor's work has been proposed in this chapter. In your congregation, would this contribute to efficiencies, or would it be more cost and trouble for everyone than it would be worth? Should your pastor make this decision, or is this an elder decision? Or a deacon decision? If such an arrangement would involve the pastor's home, how might the pastor's spouse and children be affected? Should the welfare of the family or the ministry be the highest priority? Why?

— 16 —

The Other Half

Lest we forget

A pastor's ministry to a congregation is much more than a solitary endeavor. When the pastor has a family, the usual assumption is that the family is to play some kind of supporting role. This beyond-the-conditions-of-employment expectation typically receives polite lip service, but no formality. Yet, expectations are usually much higher than the level of attention given to how the role can be achieved. The burden is usually on the family. In what follows, I am using as my example a pastor having a wife and children as typically found in so many congregations.

A pastor's life usually involves two components: the ministry and the family. They can't be separated. The responsibilities of each not only overlap, but they are interrelated, even at times interdependent. Thus, the state of a pastor's family life can have significant bearing upon the ministry. But what must also be of concern is the impact of the marriage relationship within the family and upon the ministry. I have observed that an unhappy wife can contribute to a less than effective pastor. I know this is anecdotal, but others may have observed this also. The circumstances in which a pastor's wife finds herself, can have a direct effect on whether she becomes an asset or liability to the ministry.

It has been said that a pastor's life can be a lonely life. Yet, the life of the pastor's wife can be equally as lonely, even more so. Sometimes it can be difficult for a spouse to initiate, or even to be involved in everyday relationships with others in the congregation. This is where elders can be very helpful, possibly engaging their own spouses to help arrange informal social and other events that will involve the pastor's wife. Informality can be very beneficial. Drawing the pastor's wife into the central life of the congregation will serve to enhance the potential for positive and meaningful relationships, an essential ingredient of a successful pastorate.

I acknowledge that not all pastors' wives experience the loneliness of others. In fact, many are blessed with very happy, fulfilling family circumstances and experiences. For this, we must be grateful. However, my purpose here is to encourage us not to overlook those not so blessed; to bring attention to what can be an easily ignored topic.

Is it too far-fetched to consider the pastor's wife as the "other half" of the pastor, or even in some situations, the "forgotten half?" I think not. If the marriage-ministry relationship is not a healthy one, it can cause unnecessary stress upon a busy pastor, eventually becoming a distraction to the congregation. It does not require too much imagination to see how a congregation's unfulfilled expectations of a pastor's wife, even those unspoken, can contribute to this. This may appear to be too hypothetical a possibility—an "easy blame." It can just as easily be reality. Because of the uniqueness of the pastor-spouse-congregation relationship, spousal vulnerability can be especially troublesome.

A pastor's wife can be expected to be seen at all congregational events. And the children are all too often expected not to be seen, or at least to be politely unobtrusive. "Perfect" behavior is expected. This of course will depend on the children, their ages and their dispositions. The assignment of the unofficial yet common title of "PK" to preachers' kids is not always welcomed by the recipients. PK is a pigeon-hole into which pastors' children are permanently assigned from childhood to adult, like it or not. However, as they grow older it can become a badge of merit suggesting that they had survived the challenges and risks of being a pastor's child. (I have been aware of this first-hand, as my wife grew up as a PK, and she survived!) How a pastor's children respond to the challenges will be related to how they are treated, something that should be kept in mind by elders and others alike.

A similar but typically unspoken social designation can be unwittingly (or even intentionally) assigned to a pastor's wife. "We never see her when there is something to be done." How she is perceived can depend upon how she is treated. And how she is treated can depend on how she "performs" those unwritten expectations. This suggests what may be unavoidable and interdependent causes and effects, just as it may with the children. Many factors will determine how a pastor's wife and children interact with the congregation, just as they will within their own family. Each family, each congregation and each situation is unique.

Just as elders must attend to a pastor's personal welfare, when a family is involved that same concern must also extend to the family. The first thing to recognize is that the family's role in a local ministry is usually unscripted and never defined. It is just supposed to happen. A positive contribution to the congregation is always expected, and when provided, is often under-appreciated—even criticized. But it need not be that way. Acknowledging this is a good place to start.

Instead of beginning with a "this is how it should be done" approach, elders could engage the pastor in an informal conversation as to how the pastor's wife and children might want to be involved within the congregation. (This is a question our elders ask of new members after they have been admitted into church membership in my congregation. It is asked as an invitation, not as a directive.) Ideally, this might be done during the pre-employment pastoral interview process. Including the spouse, or even the entire family, in some of the interviews will provide an opportunity to establish mutual respect for the issues involved, and to agree upon some reasonable approaches to circumstances that could arise. If the pastor has already been employed by the congregation, the annual review can also present a comfortable, non-threatening conversational venue (See ch. 14, Accountability).

It is very important to understand that the role of the pastor's wife in the congregation is unlike that of many other professional families. A doctor's spouse may be expected to show up at an occasional social event at the medical center. The banker's spouse may serve as fundraising chair for the local community foundation. The college president's spouse may be expected to host the annual spring faculty reception in the family's home. These examples are rather typical of normally predictable, easily defined and scheduled spousal roles. They can sometimes be more ceremonial than meaningful. It doesn't work that way for a pastor's wife.

The pastor's wife is expected to be "on call" whenever the phone rings and a substitute Bible school teacher is needed; when the missionary society needs a place to meet tomorrow night; or when asked to organize and be responsible for running this summer's Vacation Bible School. These kinds of requests are neither predictable nor easily avoided. This is just what happens. The spirit of the response is likely to be similar to the spirit in which the request is made. A more comfortable interface will be possible if the elders have paved the way for these expectations. Just as a pastor's wife may be expected to respond quickly and positively to these types of unpredictable requests, the elders and the congregation must also understand that there will be situations where this is neither possible nor appropriate.

It is a good idea to have a few guidelines in place. A pastor's family should not be subjected to the impulsive expectations and requests made by individuals, especially when they occur outside the normally accepted congregational structure. Informality can be a virtue, but such individually and spontaneously generated requests can produce unexpected responses. Some will be regretted. Each will have a consequence. A "yes" may suggest a soft touch, when it is really a result of not knowing how to say "no." A "no," because of something personal that should not require an explanation, may be interpreted as an unwillingness to help. Either misunderstanding could be avoided if some guidelines are in effect. This is not to suggest a prescriptive approach to personal conversation or spousal behavior. It is, however, a suggestion that there be some understanding within the congregation that the pastor's family is not fair game for every task, especially for the tasks no one else wants to do. This kind of caution may seem a bit too idealistic and impossible to achieve. Yet, as with most things, if it is never given an opportunity to work, it never will.

Anticipating and preparing for these kinds of situations should not be difficult. One suggestion is to establish some general guidelines whereby any invitation to a pastor's spouse to assume a new responsibility is legitimized by extending it through some "official" source such as a committee chair. This procedure could also apply to requests made of other members of the congregation as well, thus not making the pastor's family obvious targets of the guidelines. If this is too formal an approach, another less official option might be useful. If the pastor has an office assistant, perhaps that person could serve as screener. Still too officious?

At minimum, a concept of "respectful intrusion" into the family's personal time should be encouraged by anyone seeking help. Without too much trouble this approach can be proposed to the congregation by the elders.

What about the PKs? Once again, depending on their ages, their personal lives may not always be their own to share. The younger ones should be approached through their parents. A more direct approach becomes appropriate as ages progress. The age of independence will be unique to each, thus prescribing how to deal with this defies a generic approach. Being alert to, and respectful of the child is called for here. Good judgment should prevail.

One last thought about the forgotten half: I have been aware of programs for pastors' wives that have been held while the pastors attended a conference or other meeting at the same site. These were typically arranged so the wives could discuss issues by themselves that were related to their own personal experiences, roles in the ministry and the life of the congregation. Unfortunately, this kind of arrangement can suggest the appearance of simply providing something for wives to do—a type of "adult busy-work" while the pastors attend to the "important things" of the church. Yet, accompanying their pastor-spouses to a meeting shouldn't require a day of just sitting around reading a book while waiting (or shopping).

When meetings for pastors include more deliberate attempts to provide meaningful spousal events, and even if they are included in the general printed program, there still remains the danger that they can be seen as being of lesser importance, even patronizing. I have a different take on this.

My experience talking with women who have attended these kinds of meetings for pastors' wives, has made a number of issues very clear to me. Pastors' wives can be very lonely people. Their frustrations are many, and very similar to those of their peers. There is reluctance (even intimidation) for them to seek help from members of their congregations about personal issues that exist. Peer interaction and support is craved. Opportunities to meet with peers are infrequent. Gatherings where pastors' wives do get together tend to be relatively brief, leaving a desire for more time. And meetings often end without a meaningful closure or a feeling of having accomplished anything other than talk, as important as that is. So, what is the answer?

I propose that serious attention be given to addressing these very real and personal issues. This should start with the elders of every congregation recognizing the need, hopefully before it becomes a destructive factor in a pastor's marriage or more broadly within the congregation, and then finally taking some action. What I am proposing is something very special for the pastor's spouse. It can be either a local congregational effort, or one sponsored by several congregations or even by an entire denomination.

There is nothing that requires a meeting for pastors' wives to always be held concurrently with a meeting of pastors. In fact, it can be wise not to wait for such an occasion. A stand-alone conference can be very useful, even of greater value. It would increase the visibility of the event while drawing greater attention to its importance and an acknowledgment of the needs of pastor's wives.

These kinds of events don't happen very often. The reason may be more a lack of treating the pastor's wife as a priority, than an unwillingness to show the kind of love and respect deserved. It could also be a consequence of what is usually, and understandably, a pastor-centric environment surrounding gatherings of pastors.

Although the suggestions below are for elders, there is no reason elders need to go beyond encouraging and providing support for pastors' wives who may desire to organize their own event. In fact, there may be great wisdom for the elders to stay out of the way once they have demonstrated their support. Who better to plan such a conference for pastors' wives than pastors' wives?

Regardless of the role the elders play, I suggest that the following be considered.

1. Treat the issue seriously.

2. Identify problems before they arise. Recognize, acknowledge and understand the unique role of, and stresses upon pastors' wives. This

can be done by consulting informally with them. Their messages will be very similar.

3. Show confidence in those most closely associated with the issues by forming a group of several pastors' wives who can identify the most pertinent topics needing to be addressed.

4. Some topics might include:

    - Helping children cope with their involuntarily assigned PK designation; living their roles
    - Getting beyond the feeling of being the forgotten half
    - Expectations of a pastor's wife versus reality
    - Locating peer support
    - Knowing when and with whom confidences can be shared
    - Asking for help without appearing helpless or demanding
    - Managing marital stress and tensions; where and how to get help
    - Defusing the pastor's stress without creating more stress for either spouse
    - Managing personal burdens without compounding pastoral burdens
    - Dealing with the "consequences of absence" while the pastor attends the all-to-frequent evening meetings
    - Knowing how to respect the line between expressing spousal interest and spousal support, without learning/knowing "too much" about matters involving others in the congregation
    - Maintaining confidences
    - Knowing how and when to say "no" to unreasonable and inconvenient requests
    - Being a pastor's wife and a member of the congregation—living the difference

- Managing tension between the time demands of family and ministry
- Exercising patience; being realistic about its limitations
- Knowing when, and when not to speak up on behalf of the pastor
- Family finances

5. A conference goal and subordinate objectives should be established.
6. Determine supporting topics
7. Group topics under appropriate, general topical headings so they can become the foundation of a truly meaningful conference. Under each heading, arrange the topics in a sequence that will permit logical progression of thought, from one topic to the next. Prioritize general topical headings in like manner.
8. Determine the length of time required for proper attention to each topic, including how it would best be addressed (formal or informal presentation, large- or small-group discussion, etc.), then decide how much total time will be required to conduct a meaningful conference. Eliminate the topics of least value as may be required to use the available time most efficiently.
9. A full-day, or longer, conference program will attract greater interest than if only a half-day is available. This will allow a more comprehensive program than one consisting only of a single morning or afternoon of one or two "hit-and-run" lectures. Anecdotal reports from pastors' wives confirm that substantial time for interaction is desired.
10. A format should be adopted that is conducive to producing the objectives. It should promote the best possible interaction among participants, and between topic leaders and attendees. This can be a time to ask personal questions of the leaders and for one-on-one conversations among attendees. An informal "high tea" feature within a larger program can encourage conversation.
11. As every conference must depend upon local conditions (e.g., a suitable venue and staffing, attendee travel time, lodging

requirements, food service, and general conference expenses), it is difficult, beyond generalities, to recommend many logistical specifics. However, there are a few suggestions that may be helpful.

- Strive to make attendance costs minimal, at least affordable, and even cost-free if possible. Respect should be shown to those from families not normally able to afford such experiences. The less the cost, the greater will be the incentive to attend. The entire cost of the conference could be underwritten as a ministry of the sponsoring congregation or denomination.

- Consider arranging for a conference site that has an ambiance of sufficient quality (even a vacation atmosphere) that will provide an experience that normally might not be available to attendees. This has proven to be a value-added component of similar conferences.

- Make certain that quality lodging is available for those coming from a distance, and for all attendees if the conference involves more than one day.

- Select a conference location away from the local distractions of family and other daily responsibilities, but close enough to allow a quick trip home in the event of an emergency.

- Consider providing daycare at the conference site. However, discouraging mothers from bringing other than infant children might be wise. Be aware that having any children nearby will present a distraction. This might be an opportunity for a child care stipend to be made available for those preferring to leave children at home.

- Make certain that the quality of meals and snacks will have a special appeal to those who may not have opportunity to "eat out" very often.

12. Arrange the program to have a generous amount of topic-focused small group discussion.

13. Speakers and/or discussion group leaders who will be included on the program should be selected carefully and assigned topics as far in

advance as possible. They should be advised of the conference objectives.

14. Some creative thought could be invested in the possibility of structuring a program that does not depend upon "outside" speakers. Limiting speaking and other group leadership roles to the attending pastors' wives, especially those who are experienced in their roles, is an idea worth considering. A willingness to share personal, intimate, revealing and even embarrassing issues might be more likely by those attending.

15. Allow a generous amount of "down time" for self-directed informal conversations throughout the program (e.g., thirty-minute breaks).

16. Distribute a program ahead of time, possibly including pre-conference reading assignments, topics and questions for later discussion.

17. Limit attendance to pastors' wives of the sponsoring congregation or denomination. The conference should not be viewed as an "anyone come," more general women's conference. This will acknowledge the common experiences, concerns and backgrounds of those who attend. It will allow attendees to be more comfortable as they share their concerns with those of like-mind who may have found solutions to similar challenges.

Question: What should be the elder's role in all of this? Answer: To recognize and to be sensitive to the need! And to help, even leading when appropriate in the development and implementation of any plan that encourages respect for the pastor's wife and the entire family. Elders do not have to be unnecessarily involved in planning this kind of event, but their position of leadership in the congregation assures the opportunity to be catalysts for whatever action may be helpful.

Much of the preceding applies to pastors too. Pastors get lonely. They get discouraged. They also need and often crave peer support, especially those who serve in remote locations. I once heard it stated by a pastor speaking on the floor of an annual meeting of the denomination, that a major benefit of attending such meetings is to engage in personal fellowship with peers. Essentially, this was heard as a pastor's cry for help.

This public expression of "professional loneliness" underscores the challenge for elders to provide similar opportunities for pastors as well as for their spouses. Do not forget the PKs! The need for peer engagement is not limited to adults.

From Here to Reality

1. How can elders help when there are personal issues between pastor and spouse that can become detrimental to the ministry? How can this be done without being unnecessarily intrusive, and without creating dissonance between pastor and elders?

2. Are there circumstances when the elders should leave a family problem alone by ignoring it completely? What might they be? What benefits or casualties could result?

3. What strategies might be useful when helping a pastor's children acclimate to a new congregation? Is there ever a time when pastors' children should be "out of bounds" to elder oversight?

4. Under what circumstances might the public perception of a pastor's family become of concern to a congregation? If this becomes reality, how can it be addressed without doing harm to existing relationships? What steps can be taken by the elders to help a family avoid such concerns before they become public? Is this even possible?

5. Is "the forgotten half" a fair descriptor for some pastors' wives? Perhaps there is a more helpful expression that would still direct attention to what could be a very real problem. What would you suggest?

6. Should the relationship between a pastor's family and the congregation remain unscripted, or is there benefit to some formality? Which approach is best in your congregation? If other options are more appropriate, what might they be? What are the potential pitfalls of each?

7. Should pastors' children have the same kind of opportunity for peer relationships as proposed for pastors' wives? How can elders help facilitate this?

8. Do any of the conditions discussed in this chapter relate to your pastor's wife? Are adjustments needed in your congregation? If yes, what might they be?

— 17 —

Physical Vitality

Physical fitness is not just for the other guy

In many respects, pastors are no different from the rest of us, especially when it comes to exercise. Some are dedicated to physical fitness as a way of life. At the other extreme are those who simply cannot find the time for such a thing. This suggests a wide continuum along which can be found our pastors—and ourselves! It is undeniable that we need not look too far before it becomes painfully obvious that not all pastors appear to be inclined toward the athletic life. Some can be found all too near the no-attention-at-all-to-physical-fitness end of the continuum. This cannot possibly contribute to a vital pastor.

I have come to believe that physical fitness has to be a very important component of the pastor's life. I have not arrived at this conclusion because of a personal commitment to exercise, but simply as a result of years of casual observations. I have known pastors who make time to run many miles a week and attend to careful diets. Some find time to be on the basketball or handball courts on a regular basis. Others appear to have been firmly affixed to their desk chairs and to their love of good food.

I was once involved in organizing a two-week revitalization program for pastors that was primarily academic in nature. Almost as an afterthought, a small exercise component was added primarily as a diversion to the daily routine, and also to see if it might draw attention to another dimension of revitalization. A personal trainer was engaged to prescribe an exercise routine unique to each program participant. Much to the surprise and satisfaction of all, even for the pastors not so inclined, this turned out to be a highlight of the program. There must be a message here.

It has become increasingly common for some corporations, and other employers such as colleges and universities, even health insurance companies, to offer free access to exercise facilities for their employees and insureds. The reason is simple. Economics! Studies have found that healthier people are more productive, and their health care costs less expensive. Might this be a good example for a congregation to follow?

Looking around the room at most church gatherings suggests that pastors are not alone in their lack of attention to physical fitness. Elders are not always physical fitness models for the pastor. Thus, how can the "elder-pot" call the "pastor-kettle" black when advising on the topic of fitness? This is a good opportunity for elders to apply to themselves, what is recommend for their pastors. However, given the focus here on pastoral vitality, the emphasis in what follows will remain on the pastor.

Each elder accepted a noble task when the office of elder was assumed. The task should extend beyond things spiritual, and beyond those that are more easily observed as being associated with the congregation. It should include matters related to the pastor's daily health and vitality, including physical activity and fitness. These are all of direct significance to the welfare of the congregation. There are things the elder can do, none of which go far beyond common sense. The biggest problem may be that the "common senseness" of it all makes them too easy to ignore. It is properly assumed that pastors take care of a lot of things for themselves, especially those that are more personal. As correct as this may be, it cannot always be assumed when it comes to exercise.

There are at least three likely impediments that can be expected to discourage a pastor or anyone else from starting an exercise or fitness regimen: making the commitment; arranging for the time required; and being willing to commit the financial means necessary should there be a related cost. The first may be the most difficult, although the least expensive. An additional impediment could be that many of us just don't like exercise. This includes me, but I do it anyway. This is where compassionate encouragement and education should become a new and possibly unanticipated responsibility of elders. For some elders, helping the pastor with this can be a natural and even enjoyable personal engagement.

Short of demanding that a pastor agree unwillingly to a physical fitness routine, there are several approaches that can be effective. These range from including such an expectation within the original employment agreement, to the other extreme of after-the-fact, casually suggesting (or even insisting) that the pastor include time for physical fitness in the weekly schedule. Lying between these two approaches are options that may be more acceptable and have a greater probability of success. Any one of the following suggestions, or any combination of one with another may suffice.

1. If not initiated voluntarily by the pastor, the importance of including a block of regularly scheduled time for personal physical exercise within each week's schedule should be encouraged. If necessary, this can be stated as an expectation.

2. Ask the pastor to prepare a self-defined weekly exercise program.

3. Request that time committed to exercise be acknowledged in the monthly pastor's report to the elders. (See ch. 14, Accountability.)

4. One or more elders, or another member of the congregation so inclined, might invite the pastor to a weekly game of tennis or other sport.

5. Arranging for a small group of local pastors to gather together occasionally for some type of regular fitness activity might be considered.

6. It could be helpful for the pastor to schedule a meeting with a licensed trainer who would prepare a personal exercise plan. If it becomes an issue, and as an encouragement, the cost could be assumed by the congregation within the budget as a "pastoral expense" or fringe benefit.

7. Although more expensive, the engagement of a personal trainer may be the best means of producing a desired physical fitness goal. It may also be the most efficient option when time, expense and results are compared. Again, this is a good item for inclusion in a fringe benefit package.

8. If it is best that the pastor purchase a membership at a local fitness facility, this option could be incentivized by using congregational funds for sharing the cost, or even assuming the entire cost. With proper planning, this option could also be included in the pastor's original employment fringe benefit package, but if it is too late for that, included later in the annual budget.

9. Benefits beyond those for just the pastor will be realized when the pastor's spouse and other members of the family are included in any of the above options. In addition to the obvious physical benefits, family memberships may lead to reduced health care expense.

It should not be difficult to recognize that there is likely a direct relationship between a pastor's physical vitality and that of the congregation. Empirical evidence is all around us. There is no need to wait for extensive research on this one. Vital pastors, vital churches!

From Here to Reality

1. If you are an elder who does not enjoy exercise, how can you get beyond your own disinterest, and help your pastor who also resists exercise? Is there not a message here for both pastor and elder? Does this present a problem or an opportunity?

2. Would it be feasible to develop an exercise program that includes both elders and pastor? How might this be received among your elders? Would this make your pastor feel pressured? What about your elders? Could it become a welcomed form of comradery? Or could this be seen as an unnecessary intrusion into a very personal topic? Is attention to a pastor's physical exercise really worth the trouble?

3. Do you agree that a direct relationship exists between healthy pastors and healthy churches? If the relationship might not always be seen as being so direct, what are some ways this could develop into problems for a congregation? Is it possible to prevent this? What are some other issues related to physical fitness that also need to be considered?

4. Is it proper to view a pastor's physical fitness as an economic issue?

— 18 —

Team Ministry

Sometimes one plus one can equal three

A team ministry (two-pastor or multi-pastor pastorate) can present some difficult challenges, especially when assigning closely related responsibilities. Be assured that many of the topics addressed here, especially relating pastoral strengths to specific ministry responsibilities, will also apply to the congregation having only one pastor. However, by way of illustration, my focus is on a two-pastor pastorate.

The synergism that can be possible, and normally expected when two pastors work closely together, requires very careful, discrete and unbiased planning. To do otherwise is to contribute to a dilution of each pastor's potential, the opposite of what is desired. The necessary planning required by elders should occur even before the new pastoral relationships begin. The plan must be fully understood at the beginning, not after problems have occurred. Planning after the fact only adds unnecessarily to what can already be a big challenge.

It is important that the congregation make the most efficient use of its investment in its ministry team. This must not be restricted to preaching, but must extend to all aspects of the work: outreach; member visitation; ministry expansion through new works; visionary planning; educational programs; diaconal ministries; and interactions with the immediate community. This may require objective re-thinking of how a congregation currently functions and what changes might be helpful and appropriate.

The Basics

This will be a significant undertaking. It must be done properly. I recognize that having two pastors, especially in a smaller congregation, may be impossible because of limited resources. Yet, where this is possible, essentials include a supportive and eager congregation; a carefully thought-out plan that anticipates challenges; ideally, pastors respected within the congregation and throughout the denomination; pastors who respect each other; and unified elder leadership and enthusiasm for implementing this type of ministry. Significant ingredients must also include pastors having amicable personalities, complementary abilities, commitment to existing ministry objectives, evidence of previous personal accomplishments and a true desire to be part of a successful team ministry.

The Challenges

The greatest potential of this kind of pastorate may also present the greatest challenge—integrating and implementing pastoral strengths. If this is not handled properly, the full potential of a synergistic relationship will never be realized. The congregation's existing "efficiency plateau" will become permanent, a lost opportunity.

The challenge becomes even greater when the pastors' personal strengths are applied to and integrated with the short- and long-range objectives of the ministry. Strengths must be coordinated in a manner that strengthens, not weakens, what currently exists.

As uncomfortable as it may be to admit, perceived personal turf issues, competing strengths, possessive desires and demands of one or both pastors can become deal breakers. There is little that can become more destructive to the potential of a two-pastor pastorate than a pastor constantly "looking over the shoulder" at the other pastor. Nothing short of direct, meaningful and decisive preemptive discussions between the elders and the pastors can avoid these kinds of issues. This potential for problems must not be left unchecked or ignored.

An always present easy way out would be to let the pastors figure it all out by themselves, self-selecting which responsibilities each would prefer to assume. Just as water seeks the lowest level, the potential for each pastor to seek what suits best can lead to a lower level of total effectiveness. Even if there was perfect amicability between pastors, the art of sharing could quickly change into unartful competition. This possibility is not worth the risk. From the beginning of the relationship, a moderating influence needs to be present in the form of elder oversight, leadership and discretion.

Only when the goals and objectives of the ministry are agreed upon by the elders and pastors, can success be possible. Compromise and rethinking of convention, both individually and collectively, yet without compromise of either doctrinal or ethical integrity, also may be required. Elders who may have been in the congregation longer than the pastors, must not think that change is unacceptable. Congregations experience change over time. Some change is good, some not so good. Elder responsibility includes the visionary leadership required to stay in front of change, and even to create it when it would be helpful. Responsible leadership requires constant monitoring and possible adjustment of existing short- and long-range plans and the vision to define new or revised objectives. This is essential in a team ministry.

Some Things to Consider

I will not attempt to be specific on matters related to numbers, time frames and other issues that will be unique to local congregations. Yet attention to some of the following functional generalities and how they are related to team ministry assignments will help.

The congregation must be well served, and neither caught by surprise nor threatened by new and occasionally changing pastoral assignments. Regular attention to the need for keeping the congregation abreast of proposed change is wise. This can be accomplished by providing regular progress reports through electronic, verbal or printed communication; also, by including some lay members of the congregation in the planning process. Good, regular communication on all matters, not just pastoral responsibilities, will serve to reduce anxiety and unnecessary rumors and misunderstandings. It will build confidence in the plans being developed and in those responsible for the planning.

Finances will always be of concern, the cost of two pastors being an obvious issue. A good plan that carefully presents the cost versus benefit of having two pastors will be very important. There should be a comprehensive three to five-year-plan for, and understood by, the pastors clearly related to congregational mission, goals and objectives and the cost of achieving them.

Congregations, especially smaller ones, occasionally look to other congregations for help. It is reasonable that a congregation having two pastors, should be prepared to occasionally and temporarily share their pastors with other congregations when legitimate needs and opportunities arise.

This is a good place to be reminded of the relationship between a congregation and its denomination. With the assumption that vital pastors contribute to vital churches, it is also safe to assume that vital churches will contribute to vital denominations. The relationships are real, obvious and direct. Thus, this reminder: the ministry of the larger Church is an extension of the local church ministry.

The local congregation must be careful that it is seen as neither a "soft touch," nor as being unnecessarily protective of its pastors and other resources. Legitimate calls for help can include requests for preaching assistance, moderating elder meetings in other congregations during absences of pastors, membership on denominational committees and commissions and helping with other denominational programs (e.g., youth ministries, overseas missions, etc.).

The acceptance of each external request for assistance must be carefully coordinated with the elders. This remains true whether the request comes from another congregation or from a parachurch organization. Special attention must be given to regular responsibilities, immediate needs of the congregation and the personal schedules of each pastor. This is where elders will need to recognize and exercise an easily overlooked role on behalf of their pastors — helping them to say "no" when necessary, and "yes" when appropriate. In some circumstances, elders may need to "protect" their pastors from accepting invitations beyond what is reasonable. In others, sharing a pastor may need to be encouraged even though this may create unusual pressures on the team ministry and the congregation. In either situation, matters such as mission, workload and congregational budgetary implications must remain central as the elders provide their counsel. Most routine denominational assignments should be addressed in the same manner, but always with respect for the needs of the local church as well as the larger Church.

The educational programs of the congregation (e.g., classroom teaching; youth, college and young adult ministries and related activities; Vacation Bible School, Bible studies, etc.) must be a focus of elder attention when making assignments within a team ministry. Preparing for teaching can become difficult when there is a weekly sermon to be prepared also. Special attention must be given to the time required for each, as well as to the actual time for teaching. It is important that pastors are visible during, and even responsible for, some of the programs in which they may not have teaching responsibilities. The dedication of pastoral time to teaching must also involve careful attention to matching each pastor's specialty with the intended audience and with the desired outcomes. Elder awareness of this is very important when considering pastoral assignments.

Assigning preaching responsibilities may be the challenge requiring the greatest sensitivity and discretion. A team ministry must begin with a carefully thought-out plan reflecting attention to a pastor's most important responsibility—preaching the Gospel.

Each pastor should be given the opportunity to exercise skills in a manner that best exhibits personal strengths. But how should the strengths and weaknesses of one be integrated with the strengths and weaknesses of another in a way that does not cause disappointment, discouragement, or even animosity? Preaching assignments require that the purpose of the specific preaching opportunity be central to any decision.

The following procedural criteria should be considered carefully.

1. Neither pastor can be viewed or treated as inferior, either by the elders or by the congregation (except as realities such as experience, professional maturity or other obvious personal strengths or weaknesses may dictate).

2. The two pastors must be respected for their individual gifts, their unique personalities, experiences and strengths, including preaching styles and methodologies.

3. The interests, potential effectiveness with a particular topic, availability, audience needs and a pastor's desire to address a particular topic all should be factors used when determining preaching and other speaking assignments.

4. If preaching schedules involve morning and evening worship services, preaching appearances should occur according to some reasonable and meaningful criteria (e.g., by topical strength, pastoral availability, sharing of responsibility, etc.) and not necessarily by a regular alternating morning-evening rotation, permanent morning-evening assignment or by some other mostly mechanical or unnecessarily subjective routine. A permanent morning-evening arrangement could imply and encourage an unintended superior-inferior view of the pastors by the congregation.

5. There is always some wisdom in maintaining consistency, especially given the desire of many to be able to anticipate events before they occur. This is human nature. Congregants usually like to be able to anticipate who will be preaching before arriving at a worship service. This can be addressed easily. By planning in advance who will be preaching at a particular service and on what topic, this information can be announced in the preceding week's printed worship program. Even better, with adequate planning, this can be made available to the congregation several weeks in advance, even a month in advance. An argument can be made for not falling into a scheduling rut that could encourage complacency by either pastors or congregation. This is not to suggest that an unanticipated appearance and or an unexpected sermon topic will not be helpful on occasion. It is simply a reminder that everyone can enjoy a little change once in a while, even in the church.

6. Prescribing an ideal approach to this issue certainly cannot be done from a distance, thus a final and proven recommendation is impossible here. There may be no perfect solution. Much will depend on many factors unique to local circumstances. The most important thing may be to be alert to potential opportunities and problems, and to be prepared to make changes as needed.

7. Pulpit appearances must not be viewed as prizes, some kind of reward or definition of status.

8. Two pastors on the sanctuary platform at the same time, one presiding and one preaching, can be an option. But there should be a well-thought-out rationale for this arrangement in order to avoid the appearance (or reality) of a tag-team approach to ministry; or one pastor being in a permanent supporting role for the other. Yet, there can always be good reason for this approach. Pastors can share responsibilities for various parts of the service including for example, the announcements, the call to worship and welcome, an invocation, an intercessory prayer, Scripture reading, a children's message and the sermon.

9. There is wisdom in making preaching assignments when elders and pastors are both present, rather than leaving it be worked out by the pastors alone, or the elders alone.

One of the greatest assets of a congregation is its preaching team. This asset must not be wasted by an unwillingness to make difficult and appropriate decisions.

Accordingly, the elders must take a good hard look at the difference between what exists and what is desired. This requires being reminded once again, that the strengths of each pastor must be related directly to the short- and long-range objectives of the congregation's mission. It is the elders' responsibility to be certain that each pastor receives and assumes the appropriate assignment. Poor assignments will contribute to inefficiencies, wasted resources, missed opportunities, and quite possibly, ministry disrupting friction.

As difficult as it may be, it is essential to candidly consider as objectively as possible, the strengths of each pastor. The following examples are presented as hypothetical strengths. They are intended to be neither comprehensive nor exhaustive; simply illustrative of some selected desirable qualities. A strength of one is not to imply a weakness of the other. Weaknesses or shortcomings must not be allowed to cloud the process. Assessing strengths as illustrated below, can be accomplished in candid conversation between elders and each pastor. Consider the strengths of Pastor A and Pastor B.

Pastor A: wisdom; vision; administrative skills; pastoral experience; excellent with numbers and financial planning; excellent at understanding and explaining Scripture, theology and doctrine; sound preaching; respected within the denomination; patient—understands the virtue of good timing; a good counselor and confidant; willing to address difficult matters; commitment to outreach ministries

Pastor B: a unique blend of scholar, athlete, historian and theologian; sound theology; expressed love of teaching and preaching; a unique and effective pulpit charisma; good conversationalist; understands the community and its sociology; a Pied Piper-type who young and old enjoy being near; boundless energy; effective discussion group leader; keen interest in contemporary social events

In order to use the combined strengths of each pastor in the most efficient and synergistic manner, elders must be willing to make the primary strength of each central to planning. In the above examples, Pastor A is the administrative visionary; Pastor B is effective in community relations. Thus, one might be the best to lead in organizational matters that strengthen ministries within the congregation, whereas the skills of the other could be most useful helping with oversight of local outreach programs. It is best to focus on the most obvious applications of talent, at least when getting started.

If each pastor is good at the same thing, it may be necessary (and best) to assign that one thing to only one of the pastors, not to both. This could easily apply to teaching or preaching.

A few, very general, broad-brush illustrations of how pastoral assignments and responsibilities could be made using the preceding strengths of Pastor A and Pastor B follow.

Administration and Planning: Pastor A

Pastoral Visitation: Pastor B

Community Outreach: Pastor B

Special Programs, Speakers, etc.: Pastor A

Vacation Bible School Administration: Annual rotation between A and B

Community Liaison and Leadership: Pastor B

Youth Leadership: Pastor B

Denominational Relations: Pastor A

Church Membership Classes: Pastor A

Education Programs (formal and informal): shared assignments*

Class Teaching and Preaching: shared assignments*

*Flexibility is desirable when making preaching, class teaching and other educational-type assignments. In general, it is best to first determine the audience, then the topics, and finally who is most qualified and who is available. Each pastor's desire to address a particular audience also should receive considerable weight in making assignments. Preaching assignments should always be finalized by the elders consistent with a deliberate plan, and not on an ad hoc or casual basis unless an emergency dictates otherwise. A willingness by the pastors to accept occasional changes in preaching times and topics will help avoid tedium on the parts of both pastor and congregant.

Suggestion: Team-preaching, as well as team-teaching should be considered within a single topical series as a value-added concept. This can work very well. It can work just as well in the pulpit as it does in the classroom if it is accompanied by proper planning and cooperative attitudes.

The assignment of meaningful titles to two or more pastors in the same congregation may appear like a non-issue. Yet, if not given very careful thought, this has the potential to become a monumental problem. Consider the following theoretical scenario.

Two pastors serve together, one being older, having ministered to the congregation for forty years and having the title of Senior Pastor. The other is younger, having served the congregation for only eight years while having the title, Associate Pastor. The Senior Pastor retires. Some elders and some members of the congregation want the Associate Pastor "promoted" to Senior Pastor. Others do not. The assumption by many had been that the Associate Pastor would automatically be given the Senior Pastor title and responsibilities in the event of such a personnel change.

> The congregation, and especially the elders, become sharply divided over the matter. In a short time, tension among the elders increases as it also does among members of the congregation.
>
> A congregational call is made for a new pastor to assume the Senior Pastor position. The candidate, when interviewed, and realizing the amount of congregational animosity and stress existing among the members over the issue, withdraws from further consideration. Other pastors who were subsequently asked to consider the position, and after learning of the previous candidate's experience and becoming aware of the congregation's continuing turmoil, decline to be considered. During all of this, the Associate Pastor is openly frustrated and disappointed for not being "awarded" the senior position. Compounding the problem, is the fact that the Associate Pastor is considered by many as never having had the most desirable pastoring skills, in addition to several other concerns. A bad situation becomes worse. The Associate Pastor begins looking for another pastorate.

This should be sufficient to make the point that pastoral titles not carefully thought through can create serious problems that could be avoided in most situations.

The term "associate" as it relates to "senior," suggests a hierarchical arrangement encouraging the former to be seen in a lesser role than the latter. This encourages one to view the associate pastor position as being the first step toward moving to the next "higher" position, that of senior pastor in the present or another congregation. In the preceding illustration much of the congregation's problem could have been avoided. There are several ways this could have been done.

One way would have been to include an explicit statement of understanding in the original pastoral call and in the employment agreement that defined the roles as being separate and distinct with no guarantee of the associate pastor becoming the senior pastor in the event the position should become vacant. To change from one role to the other would then require a new pastoral call by the congregation before the associate pastor could become the new senior pastor. This approach can avoid another problem. If the existing associate pastor was not considered suitable for the new role, it would allow the congregation to have an up or down vote, providing an opportunity for the congregation to approve or disapprove of the associate pastor's performance to date and suitability for the new role. This could easily turn out to be a vote of no confidence, with the associate pastor resigning and the congregation likely ending up having no pastor for a time. This would create an opportunity to employ a more suitable associate pastor while at the same time attracting a new senior pastor. Designing a team-ministry from the "ground up" would then become a new challenge, but also a unique opportunity.

Another option would be to have designated roles reflected in the titles. For example, such titles as Youth Pastor, Pastor for Outreach, Campus Pastor, Evangelism Pastor, Co-Lead Pastor and Preaching Pastor are increasingly common today, especially in larger congregations. Use of titles that identify pastoral areas of responsibility may help eliminate, or at least help avoid, the notion of a hierarchical arrangement. However, the difference between the roles of a youth pastor and a preaching pastor, for example, will still be assumed by many to be of lesser and greater importance, respectively. This may not be a perfect solution but with care it can work.

A third solution that I have seen used with success, is to not use any designation other than simply, "Pastor." The generic title, Pastor, can be used in the formal call when a new pastor is first employed. This will have several advantages. It will avoid the hierarchical issue. It will introduce the notion that the pastoral relationship is to be truly a team effort, with each pastor being expected to support the other. It will also be an incentive to further encourage a cooperative relationship. If one pastor should leave it will reduce or even eliminate anxiety, especially on the part of the remaining pastor. In this arrangement, it is an advantage to have a clear understanding in the original agreement of how a pastoral succession would be carried out. Yet, this option is not without possible difficulties.

The successful use of a simple "Pastor" title will be dependent upon a number of conditions. It will require pastors who respect each other and who commit to working together cooperatively. It will require a willingness by the pastors not to let turf issues interfere with their respective responsibilities. It will require elders to be alert to possible dissonance between pastors. It will require a congregation and its denomination to understand and respect the arrangement, not taking advantage of what might appear to be an overabundance of pastoral availability.

A lack of any of these requirements can lead to trouble. Conditions that can defeat the purpose of a generic approach to titles include a lack of effort by one pastor; an unwillingness by one pastor to see ways of voluntarily helping the other; or a too restrictive interpretation of how elder-assigned responsibilities are viewed by the pastors or by members. Another possible downside of this approach would be that the congregation would not have an automatically available opportunity to formally review and vote on the remaining pastor's future if the other should leave. This can be avoided by incorporating this option within the original employment agreement, or within the general policies of the congregation.

If one pastor does leave, it will provide a convenient opportunity to modify the assignments of the remaining pastor. This may not be all bad. It will be an opportunity not as easily available if more specific titles had been used. Changes in pastoral responsibility that may have been desired previously, can then be made in a less contested environment during the transition. Of course, when a new pastor arrives, the effort of integrating the skills of both pastors must begin anew.

Regardless of how titles are assigned, the message is the same. Elders must be certain to assess very carefully the consequences that can occur with any of these approaches. Some will be predictable, others not. Some will be positive, others not. This calls for great care and discretion when recruiting and selecting a new pastor for a team ministry.

In summary:

1. Elder leadership, influence and discretion are the most essential ingredients when planning pastoral responsibilities.

2. Elder responsibility requires visionary leadership and a willingness to react in a reasonable manner to changing circumstances.

3. There are many ingredients required for a successful team ministry pastorate that must be carefully assessed and managed.

4. The challenges and opportunities of a team ministry must be anticipated, assessed and then thoughtfully addressed.

5. Mutual agreement upon the congregational mission by both elders and pastors must be assured before successful integration of responsibilities is possible.

6. The application of pastoral strengths must be directly related to the objectives and goals supporting the congregation's mission.

7. Teaching and preaching preparation is very time consuming and must be respected.

8. The assignment of team preaching responsibilities requires great discretion as it can easily involve personal sensitivities and congregational misunderstandings.

9. A successful team ministry is dependent upon careful integration of pastoral skills and ministry assignments.

10. Denominational responsibilities should be acknowledged as part of a pastor's responsibilities and a congregation's obligation, and thus accommodated when pastoral assignments are made. A willingness to accommodate unexpected and ad hoc scheduling changes is a requisite to success.

11. Because of the complexities inherent in a team ministry, it is essential that good communication be maintained among elders and deacons and within the congregation to reduce, and preferably eliminate, unnecessary anxiety that can be produced by the unknown, the unexpected and the misunderstood.

12. Pastoral titles have consequences. They should be considered and assigned with care.

Much of this may seem like little more than good sense. But there is a huge difference between having good sense, and using it.

From Here to Reality

1. What are some of the problems and benefits of a two-pastor pastorate? How might the problems outweigh the benefits?

2. If you already have a team ministry in your congregation, is it working? If yes, how might it be improved? If you do not have one, would one add value to the ministry? What would be the first steps to take toward initiating a team ministry?

3. How could a team ministry pastorate that is not working well be dissolved? What precautions can elders take to avoid such a situation? What are the dangers of monitoring a two-pastor relationship too closely? Where and how is the line drawn between too close, and not close enough when giving attention to team performance?

4. What impact can a local team ministry have upon a denomination? Is there enough potential value that the impact can extend beyond the congregation? Should this possibility be a factor when a congregation considers employing a second pastor?

5. Must a two-pastor pastorate be dependent upon the size of a congregation? What are the issues? Which is more important when a team ministry is being considered: the size or the mission of the congregation?

6. What are some practical ways elders can prevent functional dissonance between pastors engaged in a team ministry?

7. What qualifications should be considered, even insisted upon, when elders select pastors who must work closely together? Should their spouses be a factor? What about pastors' ages?

8. How can the potential value of a team ministry be determined? What are some factors to be considered? Can they be quantified, or can they only be assessed subjectively? Is the use of quantitative data appropriate when considering the spiritual potential of a ministry? What about evaluating ministry effectiveness by quantitative means?

— 19 —

Team Leadership

Not just elders and pastors

An elder-deacon team, just as a pastoral team, also can produce synergistic results. This may seem like a given, but when it comes to planning by elders, the deacon can be all too easily relegated to a secondary role, or no role at all. Unintentional or not, it happens.

At times it may seem like deacons only have behind-the-scenes roles, like dealing with an aging sewer system, attending to the leaking roof or seeing that insurance policies are up to date. This is unfortunate. As important as these matters are, it is good that there are more easily observed reminders that deacons exist, as for example, when they are receiving the collection during worship services. This can remind members that the deacons are directly involved in the finances of the congregation. Yet, this may lead to a view by elders and others of viewing deacons as second-tier helpers, rather than as essential members of a larger leadership team. The role of the deacon should be understood by all as extending far beyond receiving the collection and maintaining the sewer. It should be an integral component of all planning, including planning that involves the details of a pastor's ministry.

Elders are to lead in setting the direction toward accomplishing the mission of the congregation, and attending to the spiritual welfare of members and the personal welfare of the pastor. Issues must be identified and goals and objectives must be set. This is where planning begins. This is also where dissonance between elders and deacons can begin: "How do they think they can do that? We have enough trouble just paying our pastor!" Such legitimate, but occasionally impulsive responses raise caution flags. The direct relationship between congregational planning and existing or future financial resources is a reality not to be ignored. Recognizing and addressing this as a mutual responsibility of both elders and deacons also must not be ignored. This is one of the places where team leadership should become an "easy reality."

As important as finances are to any planning, they should not be allowed to unduly influence the mission. Finances should support the mission, not define it. The "financial tail" must not be allowed to wag the "mission dog." To do so, is to be seduced by an all-too-prevalent conventional wisdom: "We just don't have the money." Finances can always be adjusted to meet a plan, just as objectives can be adjusted to conform to available and projected resources. This is where cooperation between elders and deacons is essential. This relationship cannot be treated as an afterthought, as easy as that may be.

I am not an advocate of deacons attending all elder meetings, even elder meetings dedicated solely to planning. Neither do I believe deacons should be left out of short- and long-range planning by the elders, especially when congregational resources are involved.

Although the roles of elders and deacons as defined in Scripture are separate and distinct, they are very closely related. The elders are to be concerned with the spiritual; the deacons, generally, with the physical of both the individual and the congregation. Yet, there are obvious areas within these responsibilities where they overlap, becoming almost synonymous, and at times being so similar as to be indistinguishable.

For example, a deacon mercy ministry can involve a spiritual component when people who turn to the church for help in meeting physical needs become convicted of their spiritual needs. When pastors and elders visit members in their homes, conversations can turn toward matters where deacons could be most helpful. Such occasions are not just opportunities for deacons to assist elders. They are opportunities for partnerships—partnerships that produce new leadership teamwork. A deacon joining a pastor during a home visit is an idea worth considering. This is only one example of where these two leadership groups can work closely together.

Caring for the spiritual and physical wellbeing of pastors, just as they care for others in the congregation, also requires that elders and deacons work closely together. It all begins with a clear understanding of, and a willingness to accept, the relationships existing between elder and deacon responsibilities and pastoral needs. How can this be accomplished?

First, there must be an understanding of purpose. This requires an understanding of the Scriptural call to each office. It also requires coordination with the congregation's mission and supporting goals and objectives. This suggests, especially in development of the mission statement, that ideally, it would have been best to have had both elders and deacons involved in its origin. This may not have been possible, as some elders and some deacons may have assumed their roles after the mission had been defined. Just as understanding the responsibilities of a congregational office is essential, so also is the need to understand the congregation's purpose.

Second, once the respective roles of elder and deacon and their relationships to each other are understood and agreed upon, it is important to understand how responsibilities can be carried out in a cooperative manner. Also, how a mutually reinforcing relationship can be achieved. Agreement on scripturally defined responsibilities and the congregational mission is one thing, but agreement on procedural matters can be quite another. Elders and deacons are still very human, occasionally exhibiting personal tendencies that may get in the way of a cooperative spirit. This requires finding a way to work harmoniously together.

Now, back to elder meetings and deacon meetings. Getting together during occasional but regularly scheduled meetings is good. This provides a forum for both learning and doing; learning about the "other" office, and doing things together. I have experienced elder meetings where a standing agenda item each calendar quarter provides opportunity for discussion of progress reports between elders and deacons. Normally, the deacons remained in the meeting until the discussion of matters specifically related to their responsibilities has been completed. This worked well.

Meeting together less frequently could be better in some situations; more frequently may be better in others. Every meeting involving both elder and deacon matters need not involve every deacon. Some meetings may be best served by only one deacon representative attending, perhaps the chair. There is no right or wrong way to accomplish this. The most important thing is that collaborative meetings be held.

There are situations requiring only deacon initiatives with no elder involvement. Deacons have their unique roles within which they should function without direction. However, when it comes to planning with and for the pastor, it is good that elders and deacons work closely together from the very beginning. It can be assumed that the elders would normally take the lead. Many activities within most plans will require resources of some kind, often financial.

I recall riding in a taxi from an airport in a city that was new to me, and where race relations were an active problem at the time. I had never visited this city before and the driver was explaining the best way for me to be alert to potential problems. This turned out to be more of a monologue than I needed, but I have never forgotten something he said. He told me that if we would just teach the kids of all races to get along in their schoolyards, when they became adults there would be fewer problems in their neighborhoods. I do not relate this here because I believe officers of the church should be treated as children. I do, because that cab driver had a philosophy that applies here also. Nothing profound; just good sense. A culture of cooperation is best started sooner than later. I believe this to be true for elders and deacons.

Just as planning for the pastor's personal and ministry needs requires cooperative leadership, so does working together in other ways. A congregation will be more confident in its leadership when a spirit of unity is observed among its officers. This applies to the little things as well as to the big things; from observing a casual conversation between an elder and a deacon during a church dinner, to listening to the elders and the deacons as together they present a new proposal for congregational action.

One way for elders and deacons to extend the benefits of their cooperation is to keep the congregation informed of their activities. This can be easily accomplished by making very brief summaries of meetings available (except for those topics involving confidential or personal matters). All meeting agenda topics need not be included; just the highlights of the meeting that will be helpful in keeping the congregation apprised of what their leadership is doing on its behalf. It does not take too much imagination to see how this can be like adding a third dimension to the concept of the elder-deacon team. It will have an effect similar to inviting the congregation to be involved as the third member of the team. The desire of a congregation to know what really goes on "behind those doors" will be respected. An environment will be created that encourages informal conversations between congregants and their leaders. Conversation can be a confidence-building medium.

Meeting summaries can be included in congregational newsletters, electronic communication or in a several-sentence summary in the weekly printed worship program. This will demonstrate that the elders and deacons want members to be aware of what they are doing together on their behalf. The best kind of communication is communication that helps avoid surprises.

Team leadership will have a very positive effect, especially when it is visible.

"If you think you are leading and
turn around to see no one following,
then you are just taking a walk."

Dr. Benjamin Hooks, Minister, Lawyer and Judge

From Here to Reality

1. Do your deacons desire to be involved in the "more spiritual" matters of the congregation, or are they content to attend primarily to the physical issues? If the latter, is this really a problem? To what extent, and in what ways should deacons be expected to work closely with elders? Who should assume responsibility for assuring a good working relationship between elders and deacons? Is there a way a congregation can encourage this partnership if it does not now exist?

2. It is easy to let financial limitations become the deciding factor when a congregation is developing plans for achieving its mission. What steps can be taken to avoid this potential planning failure?

3. Where should the line be drawn between elder responsibility and deacon responsibility? Should there be a line? What is the alternative, and how can this be managed? Or should it be managed at all, just letting circumstances dictate?

4. What are some ways to build and maintain good communication between elders and deacons? Between elders, deacons and the congregation?

5. Can a congregation be given too much information about on-going elder-deacon deliberations? What should be the limits?

6. The larger the group, the greater the possibility becomes that confidences cannot be assured. What can be done to avoid this when elder meeting attendance is expanded to include the deacons? Is this really a problem in the church?

Planning for the Pastor

— 20 —

Before Requesting Sabbatical Support

Writing between the lines

Proposal writing for pastors? When would a pastor ever need to prepare a formal proposal—a legally binding document? Answer: when applying for financial assistance to support a sabbatical leave requiring resources beyond those of the pastor or the congregation. Today we are seeing more external funding (i.e. from sources outside of the congregation) available for pastoral leaves, a refreshing acknowledgment that our pastors need periodic breaks. Pastors require occasional change just like many other professionals and, on occasion, more frequently.

This is good reason for pastors to know the techniques of successful proposal preparation. And good reason for elders to know how to help them. Time away from the pulpit is not just a-once-in-a-lifetime need. Personal refreshment lasts only so long. For the active pastor, this becomes a recurring reality. And so does the necessity of locating the resources required to support each leave.

Many pastors (like most people) have never had to write a formal proposal. They have never received the necessary counsel or instruction on how to approach the challenge. Proposal writing is not a simple task. It has to be engaged with great care, thought and precision if one expects to be successful. It requires a lot of work.

The conventional wisdom may suggest that the best way to write a grant proposal is to hire a professional proposal writer. Or in the case of inexperienced pastors, to ask an elder or others in the congregation to do it for them. Certainly, getting help should be encouraged, but not from someone who will be expected to become the primary writer of the narrative.

It is impossible for a ghost writer to prepare a proposal with the same emotion and passion as the pastor who needs the leave and the funds to support it. There is, however, a place for elders and others to help during proposal preparation. Elders might even need to initiate the process, especially when the pastor is intimidated by what can appear to be an overwhelming and taxing responsibility. Elders can and should be involved.

It is advisable that the elder role include general assistance with initial planning and help with the organizational and technical aspects of the proposal. The elder has a responsibility not only to approve the pastor's final plan, but also to provide encouragement, good ideas and even some hands-on help where it might be needed. Volunteering to help with editing is a suggestion. This kind of involvement will further demonstrate a commitment to the pastor's success.

Regardless of whether or not a potential funding source provides guidelines or specific directions, proposal writing basics for any successful proposal remain much the same. This is true even if the proposal is submitted to an individual. What follows are some very basic and essential assumptions, ingredients and steps that must be included in the process. These will in no way cover all that could be said on the topic. That must be saved for an all-day workshop.

Essential Assumptions

1. There is a "psychology of proposal writing;" convincing a reviewer to see things the pastor's way, but not while they are in the same room.

2. The written page will reveal the pastor's personality, organizational skills, care for detail, and by implication, what the pastor is "really like."

3. Reviewers are always trying to "read between the lines." What they read between the lines will be dictated by what is written on the lines throughout the proposal. Unintentional negative self-betrayal can be the result if great care is not given to this reality.

4. Misspellings, grammatical errors and typos will demonstrate carelessness.

5. Instructions must be followed explicitly: font size, organizational format, specific answers to specific questions, page limit, etc. To do otherwise demonstrates an inability to follow directions, or a disregard for those who will be reading the proposal.

6. Normally, there will be no opportunity for post-submission verbal explanation and clarification of anything the pastor has (or has not) written in the proposal.

7. The more sophisticated the funding source, the more specific will be the prescribed requirements for proposal preparation and submission.

8. Reviewers may want answers to questions even though the questions may not have been asked in published guidelines. This is because the reviewer will likely not have been the same person who prepared the guidelines.

   Suggestion: incorporate desired supplemental information concisely within the narrative at strategic locations, providing answers to the unasked questions that reviewers should "hear." Do this only when it will be an enhancement, not a distraction. Do not depend on using appendices for this, as appendices can be viewed by reviewers as dumping grounds for unnecessary information. Do not assume appendices will be read. They may not even be permitted.

9. Assume nothing about the reviewer's understanding of the pastor's personal situation or other local circumstances. Yet, do not be tempted to provide laborious and unnecessarily detailed explanations of something that can be stated succinctly. Always strive for brevity throughout.

10. A proposal that incorporates simple lists and graphs, easily understood quantitative data and short sentences instead of unnecessarily lengthy narrative, will demonstrate the pastor's resourcefulness and respect for the reviewer.

11. A proposal written by more than one person will probably look like it, and have greater potential for incongruence and inconsistencies throughout.

12. Most proposals are written at the "last minute" without benefit of careful and creative preparation, a disservice to both pastor and reviewer.

13. The pastor who has prepared the proposal will likely be competing against pastors having no previous proposal writing experience, and who have not taken the time to locate assistance or attend to the necessary refinements required of a successful proposal. Thus, careful attention to details will make the submitted proposal "stand above the crowd."

Essential Ingredients

1. A very short, descriptive, attention-getting title

2. A clear statement of the need (the problem) or situation that must be corrected or eliminated; should include validating quantitative data if available

3. A clear statement (preferably an itemized list) of the desired end result(s) or objective(s), that is, the new situation that will have been produced and will remain after the grant money has been spent

4. Clear relationships among the need(s), the objective(s), the activity that will produce the objective(s) and the funds required to pay for the activity; a budget that is carefully organized and conspicuously related to these three components

5. Only positive declarative statements; never conditional statements such as: "it is anticipated that...," "I hope to...," "if possible...," or "we believe that...." Such statements only contribute to the idea that specifics have not been researched completely and that uncertainties remain, a very common fault of many proposals. Uncertainties do not portray confidence.

Essential Steps

1. If guidelines are provided by a potential funding source, read them carefully prior to starting to write, and then follow them explicitly. It may be a bit difficult to fit the pastor's desired message into the prescribed format, but it must be done. Do not fail to address every

item requested, and only within the prescribed format. Use the identical organizational nomenclature and topical sequencing requested.

2. If at first the guidelines do not appear to permit inclusion of something considered to be essential in a particular section of the proposal, careful and creative insertion of this information elsewhere within the prescribed format might be possible without undue distraction. Do not ignore this possibility.

3. Leave any decision about what a proposal title should be until later in the writing process. That is, do not worry about a good title at first. A meaningful title will likely become apparent as writing proceeds, coming to mind as the narrative develops.

4. It is more effective for the pastor to approach proposal organization by first defining the need, then preparing the objectives, and finally preparing an action plan, in this order, rather than in the sequence often requested. Then, when writing the proposal, the three-step procedural sequence can be restated according to the sequence requested in the guidelines. This approach will force individual objectives to be written as clear responses to the need. By presenting the plan for action next, the relationships between actions and products will be very clear. This technique is very useful as it requires a logical sequence of thought. (See ch. 7, The Planning Sequence.)

5. It is usually necessary to estimate budget expenses many months or even a year in advance, given the time required for the entire proposal process to be completed (i.e., writing, reviewing and awarding). Because of the difficulty of accurately predicting costs that far in the future, it is important to clarify which budget items have been estimated, and how estimated costs were determined.

6. Validate the accuracy of all estimates. When possible, use budget estimates provided by normally accepted and respected sources. For example, it will be difficult, and likely impossible, to estimate airline travel or lodging costs that will be valid a year in the future. In situations like this, evidence showing that the budget item was estimated should be stated; also, how it was derived and by whom. No guessing. Do not be careless with this issue.

The Uniqueness of a Pastor's Proposal

Every proposal must be persuasive and compelling if it is to be funded. A pastor's proposal is no different, yet it will be written from a different perspective and for a different audience than most proposals. Some suggestions follow.

1. A proposal is not a sermon. Do not "preach" to reviewers.

2. Keep Scripture references (if any) to a minimum, using them very sparingly and only to reinforce an occasional important point.

3. Care should be given to neither over-explain a topic, nor to assume that reviewers know everything about the topic. Reviewers might actually be pastors who have been recruited for the job because they can more easily identify with, and understand pastoral matters. If possible, it is wise to inquire about the types (but not the identities) of reviewers the proposal will encounter. This is a fair question to ask of the funding source, and it will likely receive a helpful response.

4. Treat each topic as if it were being expressed directly to the reviewer in a personal conversation. Too much formality can be a detriment to good communication.

5. Assume that the proposal reviewers understand the Christian faith. Do not try to explain it to them.

6. Do not preach to the choir. Reviewers will be well aware of the perils of pastoral burnout, or they would not have been asked to review the application. There is no need to unnecessarily generalize on the problem. Stick to the immediate situation, the pastor's situation. That is, the pastor should write about the things that will be new to the reviewers.

7. Be certain that the proposed plan has the endorsement of the elders and other congregational leaders, and that this is stated unequivocally in the proposal.

8. If congregational statistics are included, it is best to respect all confidences, first sharing the intent of data use with the responsible congregational officer and getting approval when appropriate.

9. When including numbers representing the congregation, beware of possible unintended interpretations. For example, if using membership and attendance data, the pastor should be aware that a significantly smaller number of weekly attendees than members may direct attention to a problem beyond the purpose of the proposal. It could inadvertently imply an ineffective pastorate, an unintended distraction.

10. Be careful not to reference situations or circumstances from within the congregation that would prove hurtful to individuals or groups, regardless of how helpful they might be to validating the request. A good practice is to pretend that the situation described will be reported later in the local newspaper or on the internet. This will be a good test.

11. The pastor's family should not be overlooked, especially the spouse who may need just as much stress relief as the pastor. Even if not requested by proposal guidelines, referencing this is important, especially in a sabbatical plan. The one who knows most intimately of the pastor's personal life and needs, and who can assume a critical role, both as supporter and beneficiary, should be part of the plan.

12. If their ages make it appropriate, children should not be ignored in the plan. They too experience the impacts of family stress and fatigue.

13. Be careful not to blame individuals for problems. To the extent possible, focus on circumstances, not people, and certainly not by name.

14. If several pastorates have been held previously, especially within unusually brief periods of time, or if changes of denomination have occurred, an explanation may be appropriate. Without a reasonable explanation, unnecessary questions will be raised. Not helpful.

Some Other Suggestions

If the proposal is to be submitted to a philanthropic organization, locate a copy of the organization's most recent annual report so the titles and amounts of recent awards can be reviewed. There is no harm in requesting this report directly from the organization. This will help in determining if your proposal is within the range of grantor interests and fundable budgets. (Most annual reports list award titles accompanied by award size.)

1. Do not ask to read a previously funded proposal, regardless of its origin. The temptation to copy, even paraphrasing portions of award winning content, is sufficiently great that it is easy to fall prey to unintended plagiarism. It can also result in self-betrayal (recognition by reviewers that what they are reading has been seen before); suppression of one's own creative instincts; a foolish assumption that if this was part of a successful proposal, it certainly will be successful again (not recognizing that every successful proposal must be unique to be competitive); and not appreciating that writers of previously successful proposals may view their works as proprietary (as for example, including confidential plans, salaries, etc.). And who knows, a reviewer may have been the one who wrote the proposal being used as the model. Oops!

2. Consider writing the proposal in the first person. This is a good way to establish a direct relationship with reviewers when it is not possible to talk with them in person; more personal, less formal.

3. When the near-final draft has been completed, it should be read aloud. It will be amazing what is heard. Make the necessary changes. Delete unnecessary words. Add clarifications.

4. After changes are made, have someone other than the writer read the proposal, preferably someone who knows the pastor and the pastor's tendencies, but who is not necessarily well acquainted with the proposed plan. This will constitute a dry run by a person who has never seen the proposal before, and who will likely generate questions that can then be answered in the narrative before the draft is finalized.

5. Provide a realistic amount of time to write the proposal, allowing for possible illness, a traffic delay while meeting a delivery deadline or other unexpected intrusions. The unexpected will happen. It always does. Consider setting a personal deadline of at least one week, preferably two, in advance of the announced receipt deadline.

6. Deadlines are usually receipt deadlines, not submission deadlines. There is a difference.

7. Respecting the deadline is essential. Missing a deadline has been known as reason to eliminate a proposal from competition. It can also raise questions about a pastor's attention to detail.

The preceding has launched this topic only slightly above the treetops. There is a lot more to it. Many helpful resources can be found in local public and college libraries and on the internet. However, the search should be selective as most of these "helps" are quite generic, likely having been written for all comers. They may be far beyond the needs of the pastor asking for sabbatical support.

And finally, remember that the two most important people involved in the success of any proposal are the writer and the reader. Most writers do not particularly enjoy having to write a proposal, and most reviewers would rather be doing something other than reading one. Believe it! The preceding suggestions should make the tasks for both parties much easier, and thus also the possibility of greater success. But the ultimate success of any proposal is its competitive edge. That is up to the writer!

From Here to Reality

1. Is being able to prepare a successful request for sabbatical funding something that should be expected of your pastor? Is your pastor prepared? What issues can you anticipate?

2. Do you agree that there is a "psychology of proposal writing?" What if your pastor is not interested in the technicalities associated with requesting sabbatical assistance as presented in this chapter, preferring to "wing it?" How would you go about helping without alienating? Are you prepared? Can you successfully engage your pastor with a convincing argument if that should become necessary? What would you do if your suggestions are rejected?

3. A pastor must acknowledge that proposal preparation is very different than sermon preparation. What are the most important differences? Are you prepared to help critique the first draft of your pastor's proposal, identifying areas that might need refinement?
4. Should an elder be expected to help a pastor prepare a proposal when neither has had any previous experience? Are there reasonable solutions to such a predicament? What might they be?

— 21 —

Concept Development

The next step

Requesting and planning a leave from congregational responsibilities should not be an overwhelming experience for the pastor. If the process is too complex it can introduce discouragement into what should be the beginning of an exhilarating experience. Elimination of unnecessary challenges will be the first step toward success. The simpler the process the better.

Each of the procedural concepts presented in the previous chapters on Planning in the Church (i.e., the scriptural model, planning proverbs, goals, objectives, means versus ends and the planning sequence) are directly applicable to everything in this and the following chapter.

Conceptual development is more of a thought process than a planning process. It can become more time consuming and frustrating for the pastor than when fleshing out details for the larger plan. The more thought given to the reason why a leave is needed, the easier it will be to fill in the details required to achieve the desired objective(s). Careful pre-planning is the engine of effective planning.

Elders should encourage their pastors to start planning well in advance of the intended leave. At least a year in advance is best. Both have busy schedules involving things other than planning for leaves. Avoiding the pressures of time will be a major factor in establishing a good planning environment for both pastor and elder. Not to be overlooked is the positive impact this approach will also have upon others. A reasonable allocation of planning time will allow a congregation greater opportunity to be kept apprised of progress, thus reducing the potential for last minute misunderstandings.

A previously approved pastoral leave policy will contribute to a smooth start (See ch. 13, Time Allocation; Study and Renewal). This evidence of forethought will help reduce anxiety. It will allow the pastor to concentrate on preparing the request, rather than being concerned about whether or not the possibility of a leave even will be available. This is an opportunity for elders to be encouraging and supportive in what could be a frustrating time for the pastor. It should not be an exercise in seeing if the pastor can convince the elders that a leave is deserved. Encouragement and the personal help of elders in the early stages of the process will be reassuring (See ch. 25, A Pastor's Testimony).

Before anything is put in print, careful thought must be given to the true purpose of the pastor's leave or sabbatical. Yes, it is to be a break from the ministry; a time for change, relaxation and renewal, and in many respects, a vacation from the ordinary. However, it should be far more than a vacation. It is an opportunity for the pastor to grow personally and professionally. It should be an opportunity to engage in an activity (or activities) that will provide something new for the pastor; something that would otherwise be impossible.

In addition, I believe every leave should also be of direct benefit to the congregation. This is where the elders come in. Elders must help their pastors to see the bigger picture, a view beyond the personal.

The first step is to help the pastor identify and evaluate areas of personal and professional needs, establishing priorities within each. Providing discreet counsel is appropriate here. The danger of prescribing rather than advising must be avoided. While recognizing that the elders must ultimately approve the leave and the plan, to be of greatest value the final determination of goal(s) and objective(s) should be made by the pastor. A leave is a very personal event based upon very personal needs. The pastor's priorities should prevail.

As the general concept of the leave is being worked out, the benefit to both the pastor and to the congregation should be emphasized in the plan. This is called "secondary impact;" something that is also produced as a result of achieving the primary objective. It could also be called an intended consequence. For example, a longer-term secondary impact on a congregation might be the pastor's improved counseling skills available to the congregation when an advanced degree is earned. Ignoring how a pastor's leave can also benefit the congregation is to miss a very valuable component of the plan. This is another way for elders to encourage pastors to recognize their full potential. The secondary impact of any award is always very attractive to the funder.

Ideally, a simple format for presenting the pastor's plan to the elders should be available before it is needed, perhaps even at the time of initial employment. This will serve as an immediate incentive, suggesting that the new pastor will not be forgotten as soon as the study door is opened and closed for the first time. It will demonstrate a commitment to assuring the pastor's future professional growth and success.

The suggested mini-proposal format that follows provides the conceptual components of a proposal to the elders; the first step in getting local approval of an idea. It will resemble a conventional proposal, but because of its brevity, it will serve only as a framework for a more detailed presentation later. It will encourage the pastor to focus on the bigger picture; help develop an effective working relationship between pastor and elder in preparation for when the "real" proposal is written; and contribute to clarification of the pastor's current role, relating it to the congregation's mission, present and future. And most practically, its use will be a dry-run exercise in preparing for the final grant application. This will take the edge off the anxiety generated by what can be an unexpectedly overwhelming experience. Thus, the appropriateness of calling this a mini-proposal, or conceptual framework.

When compared to more formal proposal preparation, the creation and use of this format is somewhat atypical, as the people who designed it will be the same ones who will help the pastor use it. Elder participation will demonstrate a desire to help achieve the pastor's success, the ultimate purpose of the entire exercise. As with any other planning document, brevity is encouraged. It should not require more than two pages. This will keep everyone happy, especially the pastor.

Title of Proposed Leave

Inclusive Dates of Leave (months, days and year[s])

Summary of Purpose and Plan (brief; several sentences)

Perceived Need (brief; several sentences)

Goal(s) (numbered list if more than one)

Objective(s) (numbered list if more than one)

Proposed Activities or Events (numbered, sequential list)

Other People Involved (list, including positions and titles)

Expected Benefit to Pastor (list specific examples)

Expected Benefit to Congregation's Mission and Ministry (list specific applications)

Cost Estimate and Source(s) of Funding (single round figure only; not a budget; reference congregational and other likely sources of financial support if available)

Note that use of a list format is recommended for most items. This will have advantages for both pastor and elder. It will force an emphasis upon purpose, not wordsmithing. It will eliminate unnecessary concern about being grammatically correct in a narrative format. The focus will be on the plan, not the presentation. There will be enough of that required when writing a more comprehensive proposal at a later date.

This exercise will provide an efficient means of communication between pastor and elder, the foundation for future conversation when details are being worked out. It is also a good learning exercise for each, as together they experience the challenges of brevity as required when writing and reading proposals.

From Here to Reality

1. How will a pre-existing pastoral leave policy contribute to the elimination of frustration when a study leave is first being considered? Who will be helped more by the policy, the pastor or the elders? What are the possible consequences of not having a leave policy in place when a pastor's leave is being considered?

2. Who should determine the best reason for a pastor's sabbatical leave? What might be some of the factors to be considered, and by whom? When should planning begin? How can elders help the pastor avoid having a personal leave being viewed by the congregation as only a self-serving experience?

3. Are there any good reasons for someone other than a pastor to be responsible for creating the narrative of a request for sabbatical support? How would you respond if your pastor asked you to do this?

4. What are the most difficult issues a pastor might encounter when developing a conceptual theme for a leave? How can they be avoided? Are you currently prepared to help? At what point in the process should your help be offered? Or would it be better to wait until you are asked for help?

5. Can an extended vacation, with a change of pace being the only objective, be a justifiable reason for a pastoral leave? How likely is it that your congregation would agree to such a request? Could this be proposed in a manner that would receive congregational approval and third-party funding? Ideas?

— 22 —

Preparing a Request

Speaking to eyes, not ears

Preparing a grant proposal and preparing a sermon may at first appear to be somewhat similar endeavors. They are not. They do have much in common, but there are too many differences to be ignored if a proposal is to be successful.

Perhaps the most significant difference is that a proposal is read by reviewers and a sermon is heard by a congregation. Both are prepared in the absence of the consumer; but one, the proposal, is "consumed" in the absence of the writer. The advantage clearly goes to the pastor when preparing and delivering a sermon. Inflections, body language and other commonly expected delivery techniques, even unscripted verbal annotations, can be added during the presentation. When the pastor is required to prepare a proposal, the challenge takes on an entirely new and likely uncomfortable dimension. Eye contact cannot be established with the reader. It is a matter of written communication versus oral communication.

Both the sermon and the proposal must be persuasive, but for different reasons. The sermon is designed to elicit the listener's response to Scripture; a personal and spiritual response. A grant proposal is designed to elicit the reader's response to an idea; ultimately, a financial response. Each must be personal. Each presentation must be progressively persuasive, but again, sermon delivery has the advantage. The contact between the pastor and congregant is both personal and direct. The contact between the pastor and the reader of a proposal remains indirect. Only the printed page can represent the pastor, and only in the pastor's absence!

Submitting a proposal to reviewers would be like giving a printed copy of the pastor's sermon to the congregation without it having been preached. It would provide opportunity for analysis, re-analysis and even more analysis of the printed page. It would not be a catch-it-when-you-hear-it proposition. Sermon preparation assumes the listener's immediate attention to what is heard. Proposal preparation assumes that time will be available for a reviewer's delayed response, often involving consultation with others.

The sermon and the proposal must each be persuasive, compelling and personal. But how? If the sermon has all the advantages, then the proposal must make up for its disadvantages. What follows is not an attempt to make further distinctions and comparisons between sermon preparation and proposal writing. That is not the purpose here. The purpose is to concentrate on proposal organization, content and persuasiveness only. Further, it will assume that a temptation always exists for a pastor to succumb to the notion that proposal organization will simply require the same thought processes and elements that have produced successful sermons.

Applicants for most grants, including sabbatical leave grants, will often find that explicit directions and required formats are provided by funding sources, especially by those more sophisticated than others. If this is the case, follow the directions to the letter. However, for use when a specific format is not provided, an organizational format is recommended below.

But first, a few things to keep in mind:

1. An articulate, well-organized and succinct presentation is a very effective way to bring someone to another's point of view. To this end, organizational tact is essential.

2. Reviewers are susceptible to the subtleties of thoughtful persuasion. To ignore this aspect of proposal writing is to hinder the courtship between a good idea and financial support.

3. In general, the entire proposal should be single-spaced on standard 8 1/2 x 11-inch paper, using a 12-point font for the narrative. A smaller font will be more difficult to read; larger font is unnecessary and wastes space.

4. The excessive use of varying font sizes, font types, bold type and underlining, etc., will only contribute to unnecessary and often confusing distraction (Times New Roman is a recommended font type).

5. Careful presentation and alignment of items on a page (e.g., lists, charts, diagrams, etc.), and the judicious use of white space will contribute to clarity of expression and pleasing visual impact; also to quick scanning which reviewers like to do.

6. Standard one-inch margins should be used throughout.

7. Use double spacing between paragraphs.

8. Do not use color to enhance illustrative charts or anything else in the proposal. Proposals are often duplicated after receipt for use by multiple reviewers, and original colors may not reproduce well (or at all), leaving an appearance that is less than desirable. Not a good message!

9. Beginning with the Introduction, each section of the proposal should immediately follow the preceding section on the same page if space allows. That is, don't waste space by insisting that each new section begin at the top of a new page.

10. The title of each of the first three section headings of the proposal (i.e., Proposal Summary, Congregation, and Table of Contents) should appear at the center of the page. The remaining section headings can be stated at the left margin. The use of bold type for all headings will be helpful.

11. If a page limit is prescribed by a funding source, convention suggests that it applies only to the narrative that follows the table of contents, and excludes the budget. Respecting the limit will demonstrate care and attention to detail. A page limit can actually be helpful, as it will be an incentive to prepare narrative that is brief and well-focused.

12. Unless directed otherwise, the entire proposal should appear on only one side of each sheet; two-sided narrative is inconvenient for a reviewer.

13. Page numbers should appear in the upper right corner of the page making them easily seen as pages are turned.

14. The final proposal should be fastened together with only a single staple in the upper left corner. Do not use fasteners commonly found in folders for three-hole-punched pages. Such arrangements make it more difficult to duplicate a proposal if that should become necessary.

15. The use of elaborate (or any kind of) binders may suggest a lack of cost conscientiousness; not a good idea when asking for money.

The recommended outline below assumes that the proposal will be submitted as a request for pastoral sabbatical leave support, however the format can be modified and applied to other types of grant requests as needed.

Now, to the actual organization of the proposal.

Cover Sheet (or Face Page): This is the first (unnumbered) sheet of paper and should present the following information double spaced, and in list form. It is to be a stand-alone page that serves as a cover for the rest of the proposal. Only the following information should be presented.

1. Name of the organization to which the proposal is being submitted
2. Proposal title
3. Submitting pastor's name and title
4. Name of the pastor's congregation
5. US Mail address
6. Email address
7. Telephone number(s) (cell and landline as appropriate)
8. Proposed duration of funding (start and end dates; actual days, months and years), i.e., the time during which the money will be spent
9. Name and title of person to whom checks should be sent

10. Pastor's signature on a signature line immediately above the pastor's typed name. (A second signature and title may be desirable but not required; e.g., an elder, deacon or other congregational officer.)

Do not affix a specially designed cover in front of this cover sheet, regardless how attractive the congregation's logo or weekly worship program design may be. A proposal is to attract funding through its narrative expression, not because of clever attention-getting designs. Such distraction is a sign of naiveté. This is not a third grade student paper on flamingos.

Proposal Summary (or Abstract): Start at the top of the page immediately following the Cover Sheet. The proposal title should appear at the center of the page, two or three spaces below the section heading (Proposal Summary).

The summary should be no longer than three paragraphs (fewer if possible), and be limited to no more than one-half page. It should be succinct, presenting a clear overview of the entire proposal, with special emphasis upon the objectives (projected outcomes). This is to be a general summary of the entire proposal, not just the outcomes. The total dollar amount requested and the duration dates of the sabbatical should be presented at the left margin in list form, and on two separate lines following the summary. Nothing else should appear on this page. (This is the second sheet of paper in the proposal).

Hint: It is much easier to write the Proposal Summary after the entire proposal has been written.

Congregation: A description of the pastor's congregation should begin and end on the third sheet. It should include the following: mission statement; denominational affiliation; brief historic reference; specific strengths; organizational structure and staffing pertinent to the proposal; experience in administering previous grants (if any); geographic location; surrounding community; and other items considered essential to the proposal's success. This should be limited to a single page narrative, with the section heading, Congregation, appearing at the top center of the page.

Table of Contents (not an index): A Table of Contents is necessary only if the proposal narrative, excluding the budget, exceeds five or six pages. Begin this on the fourth sheet of paper. Limit to a single page with the heading appearing at the top center of the page. Following any generally accepted and easily understood style, list all major sections of the proposal narrative to the left, with corresponding page numbers to the right. Sub-sections of the narrative, if used, should only be included when space permits. Nothing else should be on this page.

Introduction: Denote this as page one of the proposal. Beginning with this section, all of the following section headings should appear at the left margin. The introduction should be a very brief overview of the problem (need), projected outcomes (objectives), and proposed plan for producing the outcomes, presented in this order. Note that this is not a proposal summary. The emphasis (different from the preceding Proposal Summary) is upon the contrast between the present and the future. This is the first opportunity to introduce, and further clarify the basic reason(s) for submitting the proposal.

This narrative should be limited to one-half page, and to an absolute maximum of one page.

Statement of the Problem (or Statement of Need): This section should immediately follow the Introduction, and on the same page. It is the first opportunity to establish proposal credibility. It must not be missed. Precisely define the problem to be solved or eliminated, limiting it to approximately three-fourths of a page or less. This must be a lucid analysis leaving no doubt that a problem does indeed exist. It must motivate a reviewer to read further to discover if a rational solution or plan to eliminate the existing problem is possible, and if it has been proposed in a compelling manner. However, no mention of the proposed solution to the problem should be made here. None! Only the problem to be eliminated. This section should contain quantitative documentation if available, but only if it will help to build the case.

Hint: this is where an emotional dimension can be added to the proposal. An easy way to do this is to present a short, dramatic vignette describing the situation to be resolved, followed by a sentence stating simply, "This describes me," or, "This describes the circumstances in which I find myself."

Objective(s): Whether this section heading is singular or plural will depend on the number of objectives in the proposal. More than five or six objectives will suggest something less than a focused plan. There is nothing wrong with having only one objective if only one is necessary.

Note that this section follows immediately after the problem statement. This is essential as it will present an immediate, and if stated correctly, a dramatic contrast with the problem. That is, once the existing situation has been vividly described, the contrast with the projected objectives will immediately pique the interest of the reviewer. It will generate an immediate interest in learning how this would be possible, thus a desire to read what follows. Many, if not most proposals are boring. This sequence will create unexpected interest. It is like knowing the end of the story before it begins, but wondering how it could possibly have happened.

All objectives describing the situation that will have been produced by the plan, and that will remain after the funds have been spent, should be itemized and presented in a numbered list. *This should not be a list of things the pastor intends to do during the leave.* Double spacing between items in the list will encourage the reviewer to focus on one at a time. The list should be preceded by a statement similar to, "As a result of the plan presented in this proposal, the following objectives (outcomes) will have been produced." This section need not include any explanatory narrative. If stated carefully, the list will suffice. It will present unexpected, but greatly appreciated clarity and focus.

Proposed Plan (or Solution, or Methodology): This section will likely be the most extensive of the entire proposal. It must contain explicit statements clearly defining the methods by which the problem will be solved, or eliminated. A logical step-by-step sequence of activities should be presented in the intended chronological order. A timetable of events should be included, relating each activity to a specific, realistic and actual calendar date. Dates may be difficult to determine in advance, but when included will demonstrate the precision with which the planning has been done. This will be an uncommon but welcomed element in this type of proposal.

Discrete use of professionally prepared charts, graphs, maps, milestone charts, diagrams, etc., can be very helpful in this section. The plan should be so clearly presented that no question will remain as to the pastor's ability to relate each element of the existing problem to a specific activity that will produce a particular desired outcome or objective. The less narrative the better. This is not easy, but important. It will provide the reviewer with an unexpectedly straight forward plan, thus contributing substantially to a uniquely competitive proposal.

The plan must convince the reviewer beyond any doubt, that the pastor and all others who will assume supporting roles, and all elements of the plan including the required resources, are the best possible for eliminating the problem as described. Each activity should demonstrate a relationship to at least one other activity, and preferably to the one immediately preceding it, and to the one that follows. The resulting synergies must be obvious. Activities described in the proposed plan must not exceed the capabilities of the pastor and existing resources, unless the need for new resources is stated clearly and included in the budget request as may be appropriate.

Rationale: The rationale can be presented in a conversational-type narrative. This is where back story detail can be included in a manner beyond the more restrictive style recommended for previous sections. More freedom to say what the pastor really wants to say without the restrictions of typical proposal writing formality can be used here. This is the pastor's big opportunity to explain, "why me," "why now," "why my congregation," "why this is so important" and "why this particular plan." It is the place to present any justification for salient points that may not, or could not, have been addressed in the previous sections. Quantitative supporting data should be added if it is available, but only if it can be presented in an easily understood, not overwhelming manner.

The pastor should anticipate questions not addressed in previous sections of the proposal, but which may arise in the mind of a reviewer. Consider carefully what they might be. Such questions should be answered before they are asked. This will demonstrate respect for a reviewer's need to have all the information necessary to make an informed decision. This is the place to pretend that the pastor is in the same room as the reviewer (not unlike when preaching a sermon to a congregation), and has the opportunity to expand on the detail of both the problem statement and the proposed plan. This is the opportunity to "speak" in a very direct manner. No rambling. No repetition. Use the first person if it will contribute to the intended emotion.

Personnel: This section may not be necessary, especially if people key to the success of the proposed plan have been included previously and adequately documented in the plan. However, if brief biographic sketches (including one for the pastor-applicant) would be helpful, this is the place to include them. Each should be limited to a maximum length of one brief several-sentence paragraph. This is not the place for résumés. If they would be helpful, résumés can be included in an appendix.

Citations: This is another section that may not be necessary. Include it only if Scripture, literature or other reference material has been included, but not cited parenthetically in the previous narrative. When recording citations, any commonly acceptable bibliographic method may be used. A numbered list corresponding to earlier parenthetical or superscript references in the narrative can be helpful. This section will eliminate the need of an appendix for this purpose.

Evaluation: This section can be the most difficult to prepare, and therefore it can also be the most poorly written. Those who fund sabbaticals always like to receive evidence that their investments in pastors' lives and ministries have been worth it. Yet, this kind of information may not always be requested. Nevertheless, demonstration of a willingness to provide this feedback has the potential of being that something extra that helps to put a proposal into the "approved stack." It will demonstrate the pastor's confidence in the proposed plan.

A reviewer can become very impressed with the proposal writer's integrity when a carefully thought out plan demonstrating a willingness to prove sabbatical success is read. This section will also demonstrate that the pastor is willing accept the unanticipated fact that some objectives may not have been achieved.

An important feature of an evaluation plan is a component that will produce quantitative evidence of success, or lack of success. However, quantifiable data is not always possible, especially in a sabbatical situation.

It is best to go back to the pastor's list of objectives (the things, changes or situations that are expected to exist when the grant money is all spent) and determine the best way to prove that, with success, each will exist when the sabbatical is over. This can be difficult as some objectives may be intangibles (e.g., a refreshed pastor, a meaningful travel experience, or the results of a stress challenge course or fitness program). Others may be more easily documented (e.g., a manuscript for a book or production of a syllabus for a seminary course). In any of these situations, effort must be made to demonstrate that each objective became a reality. Addressing each specifically, regardless of how difficult it may be to provide quantification, will go a long way toward demonstrating integrity of effort. Intangible subjectivity, for example when proving that a pastor was refreshed, could be documented, even quantified, by providing the testimonies of congregational witnesses. Producing evidence for something more tangible, as for example, a revitalization plan for a congregation, is as simple as presenting a copy of the actual plan.

As difficult as it may be for a pastor to acknowledge anything other than a totally successful sabbatical, it could become necessary to face and admit failure to produce all objectives. Things can happen that get in the way of even the best plan. A forthright analysis and admission of what went wrong may actually be advantageous. Candor will help. This is especially true if the cause was legitimate, that is, beyond the pastor's control. It could persuade the funder to provide additional funds allowing the situation to be corrected, either immediately following the leave, or during a future leave. Remember: the funder wants success also, or the sabbatical plan would never have been funded in the first place. An awarded grant is a cooperative investment in a mutually agreed upon enterprise. "Good problems" can become opportunities.

Budget: A good reviewer can often tell as much from the budget about the proposal and its writer, as from the narrative—sometimes more. It is often read, or at least scanned, before anything else. The budget must be as clear and precise as possible. No ambiguities! Always use whole dollars, rounding to the next highest dollar when necessary.

The budget should be divided into logical categories (e.g., travel, lodging, publication expenses, etc.), with appropriate subcategories as needed. A category labeled, "Other," can accommodate items not easily categorized elsewhere. It will be helpful if double spacing is used between each large category, and single spaces appear between subcategory items. It is best if budget items are identified by a sequential number appearing to the left of each item. This will serve as a helpful reference when explaining the item in the Budget Explanation. (See Budget Explanation below.)

Two-column budgets can be useful; one column listing the funds requested, with the second (immediately to the right) listing expenses to be covered by the pastor's congregation. Portions of a single expense can appear in both columns, with a possible third column representing the total of the items on the same line. Inclusion of a "Congregational Contribution" column will emphasize the congregation's commitment to the proposed plan. This is always a good idea. Even if the congregation assumes a cost, the cost is still a sabbatical leave expense. Every sabbatical expense, regardless of who pays for it, should always be represented in the budget.

A "third party contribution" (i.e., funds from a source in addition to the congregation's contribution, and the funds being requested) can further enhance the credibility of the grant application. This will require an additional budget column, representing expenses to be paid by the third-party, even though it may include only one or two items. This is an excellent way to demonstrate endorsement of the sabbatical plan by others outside the congregation.

One of the mistakes easily made is to ignore less-obvious expenses that will actually be generated by the proposed activity, but considered too small to be included. The assumption too often made is, "Oh, we can absorb that easily; no need to bother." Such things as personal local travel, use of existing office supplies, telephone and utility expenses are in this category. If funds to cover these expenses are to be assumed by the congregation, each should be included in the Congregational Contribution column. This will enhance the local commitment, while at the same time more accurately representing true costs.

Predicting and estimating these kinds of costs can be difficult. One way to deal with this is simply to add an item in the expense column called "administrative costs," or something similar. Include an amount equal to a general estimate of what the accumulated cost of the difficult to quantify items might be. This can be explained in the Budget Explanation section. Such costs are often called "indirect costs." However, be aware that this term is often a red flag to the more sophisticated funding source as it may have a policy prohibition against funding anything called an indirect cost. Thus, use of "administrative costs" may be the best approach.

Budget Explanation: This section serves to explain or justify, if necessary, how each budget item was derived—not why it is included in the budget. An explanation of an item should only be necessary when it is not clear how the dollar amount was determined (e.g., when estimating future travel or publication costs). Only items needing this attention should be included. If the proposal has been written carefully, the reason for each budget item should have been made clear in the preceding narrative. Thus, it is very possible that this section may not be needed, or if it is, that it may include only a few items. For convenience, each budget item requiring an explanation should be identified according to the same line designation (i.e., number) and description as it appears in the budget, thus not in a consecutively numbered list.

This should be the last numbered page of the proposal.

Absolute consistency must exist throughout the proposal, but should be especially apparent when the objectives, proposal plan, budget and budget explanation are compared.

Appendices: If at all possible, avoid using appendices. More often than not, they add more bulk than help. But if it becomes necessary, limit use to only the inclusion of such items as expanded résumés, copies of correspondence, and anything else that might be considered essential for the reviewer to see. Only information that could not have been included within the restrictions of the preceding narrative without creating a distraction, should be included here. Reference to appended materials should be made parenthetically within the previous narrative as appropriate.

Identify each appendix alphabetically (e.g., Appendix A, Appendix B, etc.) in the top right corner of the first page of each appendix (thus not continuing the preceding page numbering sequence). Center the appendix title at the top of the same page. Pages within each appendix, beginning with the second page, should be numbered in the same manner as the preceding narrative. A new numbering sequence should start with each appendix.

Proposal writing may seem like an overwhelming assignment, especially for the first timer. Admittedly, if done properly, it will never be easy. It will also be very time consuming. And if that were not discouraging enough, one should remember that most proposals are never funded. True!

Unlike sermon preparation, successful proposal writing will consume more than the twelve to fifteen hours required to prepare a sermon. It cannot be done in a week. It may even require months. Thus, another caveat for the serious proposal-writing pastor: start early, anticipate the delays that always seem to happen and set a personal deadline for completion that is considerably earlier than the one required by the funding source.

And the last caveat? A proposal must be written and submitted before it can be awarded.

From Here to Reality

1. One often hears "proposal writing" referred to as "grant writing." Why is this neither accurate nor helpful?

2. In its simplest form, what is a proposal? What is a sermon? What are the similarities and the differences?

3. What are the disadvantages of a proposal when compared to a sermon? Are some disadvantages more important than others? How would you provide counsel if your pastor fails to acknowledge, or is unwilling to accept the differences?

4. Is it reasonable to expect an elder to be able to provide helpful counsel to a pastor when neither has had previous proposal writing experience? Should this be reason to avoid seeking "external" sabbatical funding? What might be an alternative option?

5. In a proposal, what distinguishes the Introduction from the Proposal Summary (or Abstract)? Is the distinction really important? What are the challenges?

6. Assume that your pastor has the following sabbatical objective: "Personal refreshment and revitalization." What would you suggest to be included in the proposal that, when the leave is completed, will prove that your pastor actually returned refreshed and revitalized? If this proves to be too difficult, should you change the objective (not just the way it is worded)? If not, what can be done to address the difficulty? How would you do this without diluting the purpose of the sabbatical?

7. What is the purpose of the Budget Explanation when the preceding narrative has clearly explained the reasons for the expenses that appear in the budget? When is a Budget Explanation necessary? When is it unnecessary?

8. What are some features that should be included in a proposal that will maintain the interest of the reviewer?

— 23 —

Assuring Permanent Funding

A tool for building tomorrow

For the congregation that is financially able and is given to long-range planning, the endowment is a good option for assuring the ability to permanently invest in the professional and personal vitality of its pastors. An endowment may be something not often associated with a congregation. We often hear of large endowments, thinking they are found only in colleges and universities and related to wealthy philanthropists. These need not be the only places. Actually, institutional and other large endowments are good examples of what endowments can do. They serve a specific purpose unique to each. The most obvious difference between the very large endowments we often hear about, and one that a congregation might have is the size. This distinction should be cause for both encouragement and challenge as every endowment, regardless of size, started out smaller than it is today, but grew substantially over time. The potential for the congregational endowment is the same; it will start small, and with good management will grow much larger.

The scarcity of congregational endowments is understandable as they require a significant infusion of funds to be useful. Nevertheless, this is a unique planning opportunity for a congregation desiring to provide funds permanently dedicated to the education, continuing education, sabbatical leaves or other career enhancement and refreshment opportunities for its pastors. It should not be overlooked. An endowment can take on many characteristics and purposes, but in its simplest form it becomes a remarkably useful financial tool. It will help take much of the anxiety out of annual budget planning.

Definition of an Endowment

An endowment is a permanent fund, dedicated to a specific purpose (or purposes) by a non-profit organization (e.g. a church). It is for the exclusive benefit of the same organization. The endowment cannot be invaded for purposes inconsistent with the original intent of the fund, yet, modification of purpose can be made by formal action of the administering organization. Additional money may be contributed at any time by anyone, including friends of the non-profit.

Day-to-day investments made on behalf of an endowment may be entrusted to a financial management organization such as a brokerage, bank or other organization including a community foundation. Often, endowment funds are invested along with the larger holdings of the management organization, thus providing greater opportunity for innovative investment and the potential for a greater annual return on investment. Normally, the existing investment policy of the management firm is the basis for creating investment income. However, in some unique situations, the non-profit may be able to participate directly in the investment decisions. A small annual fee may be required by a management firm. This is typically deducted from the endowment's earned investment income. This fee is usually considerably less than the normally anticipated annual endowment income. The remaining earned income, or some portion thereof, may always be reinvested back into the endowment, adding to the invested funds, or principal.

Endowment funds, including the annual proceeds generated by the endowment, may only be spent for purposes stated in a "spending policy" established by the non-profit, in this case, the congregation. A spending policy is the congregation's own statement as to how to spend the earned income. The purposes of the endowment usually are written to allow the endowment's governing board (or delegated oversight committee) to use discretion and flexibility in the disbursement of funds as may be needed to realistically respond to changing economic times and needs. Yet, all discretionary spending must remain within the pre-established parameters of the spending policy.

Every endowment has a governing body or board, committee, or other designated group appointed by the non-profit organization. Determination of the financial manager and the investment and spending policy is the sole responsibility of this governing body. As time passes, the governing body may appoint new members to replace those leaving its membership.

In the case of a congregation, the governing body of the endowment may consist of a preexisting group from within the congregation (e.g., the finance committee, diaconate or congregational officers). Any one of these groups, or a new group of individuals representing one or more of them, could be constituted to serve as the governing body.

If the endowment outlives the congregation, endowment funds may be legally diverted by the existing financial manager to another congregation, to the larger denomination or to a parachurch or other non-profit organization. This can be done only when the purpose (or purposes) of the new non-profit are as closely related to the congregation's original spending policy as possible. It is advisable that when an endowment is first established, that the wording of the endowment document include a provision that addresses such an eventuality, thus reducing or even eliminating anxiety over the possible future termination of the endowment.

Advantages of a Congregational Endowment

1. Funds may be dedicated to any purpose at the will of the congregation. In so doing, a well-managed endowment offers some unique advantages and opportunities. In the following, I will assume that a congregation's endowment is to be focused on the personal and professional development of its current and future pastors.

2. A congregation's original purpose for an endowment cannot be easily altered by changes that may occur within the congregation's leadership or membership.

3. Present and future contributors to the endowment will be assured that their contributions will remain dedicated to the purposes for which they made their donations.

4. Contributors can have confidence in the potential for the growth and success of their investments, thus encouraging continued giving in the future.

5. The endowment will provide a stable, dependable source of financial support, protected from the uncertainties of inflation, fluctuations in congregational giving or other factors.

6. As the endowment matures, the congregation's energies can be increasingly re-focused on the program supported by the endowment, and not on an annual search for new funds.

7. As the endowment reaches a sufficient critical mass, fundraising and annual intrusions into the congregation's general fund budget will be no longer necessary.

8. A mature endowment allows inflationary program costs to be accommodated without having to engage in supplemental fundraising. The increase in endowment earned income should keep pace with inflation.

9. Endowment-supported programs can become permanent, taking on lives of their own.

Disadvantages of a Congregational Endowment

1. As with any investment vehicle there are always down-side limitations to consider. Several exist for an endowment.

2. Investment proceeds can only to be used according to the congregation's original intent as defined in its spending policy. Neither the original investment, nor the subsequent funds contributed to the endowment, nor the principal existing at any time, may be invaded for purposes beyond the original purpose.

3. Although unlikely, the potential always exists for an endowment to outlive its purpose and even the congregation.

4. The fee charged by a financial management firm will probably be more than one charged if the same funds had been invested within a larger fund pool managed by a denomination.

5. A sizeable endowment is necessary to produce a meaningful annual investment income. Thus, a relatively long timeline (even years!) may be required for a financially independent endowment-supported program to become permanently funded. However, in the meantime,

as the endowment grows, smaller amounts can be used for the early, less expensive stages of a new program. Normally, only a small percentage of annual investment income is used each year. This amount is flexible and will be determined by the investment and spending policies authorized by the congregation.

6. Slow endowment maturation can outgrow patience.

Advantages of an Externally Managed Endowment

1. A congregational endowment invested through a financial manager external to the congregation has the potential for generating greater annual income than if the funds are invested by the congregation. The potential size of the investment pool within which the funds can be invested will often produce a more consistent and reliable income.

2. The congregation's endowment can be invested with a financial manager selected from among the best available, locally, regionally or nationally. (The investment also can be managed by a denomination's financial officer if such an opportunity exists and is preferred.)

3. A financial management firm has the option to change investments quickly and easily to accommodate changes as they occur in the financial environment. Such occasional and incremental changes need not directly involve the congregation when they are made.

4. A financial management firm has a far greater potential than the congregation for accessing innovative investment opportunities, some even unique to the firm itself.

5. It will not be necessary for the congregation to spend any time tracking endowment investments, or being responsible for related administrative issues. The typical management fee would be smaller than the value of the time that might be required if a member of the congregation is involved in these details.

6. Investments will be made by financial professionals, not by novice volunteers.

7. The congregation's energies can be directed toward program management, not investment management.

Disadvantages of an Externally Managed Endowment

1. There will be a management fee.
2. Selecting a management firm could cause disagreement within the congregation.
3. Conflicts of interest could arise between the management firm and individual members.

Creating an Endowment

The best time for establishing an endowment may not always appear to be the moment at hand. Patience and respect for the congregation's—even the elders'—lack of familiarity with the concept may be required. For many reasons, not the least of which may be uneasiness due to this unfamiliarity, the tendency may be for the process to be put on a slow track.

Progress will require at least one person with a clear understanding of the potential of an endowment, and who has the perseverance and enthusiasm necessary to drive the plan forward. This may not sound very easy, but it can be. The steps are relatively simple.

There are only four basic components required to successfully create a congregational endowment: purpose; leadership; congregational commitment; and financial support. This is where elder leadership becomes very important. Quarterbacking any project involving congregational mission and finances must begin with the elders in concert with the deacons. Elders must take the lead in defining the endowment's purpose, then help the larger congregation understand and commit to its purpose and benefits, and finally engage the congregation in contributing the necessary dollars.

The purpose comes first. An endowment is not the endgame. Its purpose is to create conditions that will enable some other endgame or objective to be realized. If there is no purpose, there is no reason for an endowment. In most situations where an endowment is being considered, the purpose is already understood. The biggest challenge, and likely the most time consuming component of endowment development, will be to frame the purpose in a clearly defined statement.

The purpose statement must convince the congregation that it is of sufficient importance to deserve its support and commitment for the long haul. Further, the purpose statement must also be written in a manner to be meaningful to those who will become members of the congregation in the future. Funding a fully operational endowment will take time.

Although a statement of purpose must be unequivocal in intent, it should not include so many qualifiers as to restrict the flexibility required when expenditures are approved or when the governing board must respond to changing circumstances. This is where an attorney can be helpful to fine-tune the language.

It may take time to successfully present this plan to a congregation. Working toward this end can best be accomplished by a small group of congregational leaders led by at least one elder or deacon. Every congregation will be different. But human nature suggests some generalities common to all congregations. There will be members who will be anxious to follow their leaders without hesitation. There will be those who will require some persuasion, and others who will always need to be convinced of the need. It is a good idea to identify this latter group early in the effort, and then select a respected representative of that same group to serve on a small committee charged with developing the endowment plan. By being a part of the planning committee, this person will better understand the more esoteric features of an endowment early on, and learn the answers to questions that could otherwise be raised at a later time within a larger group. This will help to avoid the potential for unnecessary distractions when the plan is presented to the congregation.

Elder vision, leadership and oversight are essential. Treating this as educational exercise is best; educating the congregation to an understanding of the potential benefits to its ministry. There is little difference between preparing for this and presenting any other plan to a congregation. Once this is done successfully, the next step is to obtain the congregation's commitment. This may be a challenge, but can be done more easily with careful thought and planning. Some procedural suggestions follow.

1. At least one elder (preferably two) should become well-acquainted with all aspects of an endowment.

2. One elder should serve as a planning committee chair.
3. A small planning group of two additional congregational representatives, including at least one deacon, should be formed. (It is wise to make certain that any initial planning group be small, consisting of an odd-number of members, perhaps only three or five, to more easily achieve a majority vote when needed.)
4. Consultation with a qualified attorney may be helpful at an early stage.
5. As soon as a preliminary draft is completed, each elder should be given opportunity to review and comment on the developing plan.
6. Following further refinement, it is wise to share the draft with all the deacons and possibly another appropriate leadership group for further review and comment.
7. Financial management representatives should be consulted when planning has reached a reasonable level of confidence.
8. When all those involved in the initial planning process have become comfortable with the plan, it is good practice to share the draft with a slightly larger group. Any congregational committee or board most closely associated with the desire to provide for pastoral vitality would be a good candidate, even though a representative of the group may have been involved in earlier planning.
9. The endowment document could then be forwarded to an attorney for review.
10. An elder (not necessarily the planning committee chair) should be given the assignment of preparing and presenting the plan to the congregation.

    This presentation should be comprehensive, brief and persuasive. A persuasive presentation is possible only if the previous planning has been done meticulously.

There is purpose in what otherwise could appear to be an unnecessary waste of time consumed by sharing the endowment draft progressively with an increasingly larger group. Indeed, it will slow down the process. But, by doing so, most questions will have been discovered and answered earlier in the process than if they had been left for others to raise at a later time. Answers to these questions can then be included in a presentation or within the endowment document, or both. If left to be discovered during the congregational meeting, such procedural speed-bumps will become time consuming, serving as an avoidable distraction from the educational purpose of the meeting.

This method of incremental sharing of any developing plan before it is presented to the "final audience" for approval should be considered, regardless of topic or audience. It works.

In most fundraising efforts, it is important to demonstrate to current and future donors that there is leadership commitment right from the start. This can be best accomplished by requesting sizeable "up front" leadership gifts from elders and others within the congregation, and by dedicating existing congregational funds to the effort. The commitment of future gifts from individual wills and similar estate planning vehicles can be counted toward this. This approach is not unlike the initial "quiet phase" of a capital campaign that solicits leadership donations of key people within any organization before inviting others to join the "public phase" of the campaign.

It will take a sizeable amount, often far beyond the initial investment, for a congregation to realize a truly functional endowment. Yet, a congregation will never achieve this objective if it doesn't begin. Most financial goals appear ominous and sometimes impossible at the outset. Endowment building is no different. For an endowment principal to become effective, it is a good goal to estimate that a principal of approximately $1million could generate $50,000 annually. However, the minimum principal required to provide basic support for a personal or professional development program for a pastor would be approximately $250,000, generating $12,500 annually. The annual income from only a $100,000 principal producing $5,000, could allow a congregation to begin to support a fledgling program. Thus, support for pastoral educational and refreshment opportunities could begin at minimal levels, increasing as the endowment grows in size.

Attracting the funds required for a useful endowment will require serious, long-range commitment and effort. The most economical way to achieve this is by engaging members of the congregation experienced in fundraising. But, the word "fundraising" frightens many people. And the idea of actually doing it may frighten the rest of them. If this becomes a problem, the most obvious option is to acquire the services of a fundraising consultant. This will probably be the most costly approach, but it may produce the best results. Regardless of who does the work, periodic progress reports should be made available to the congregation by the elders.

From Here to Reality

1. Why are congregational endowments uncommon in the church?

2. Is fundraising, beyond the normal giving of tithes and offerings, proper within the church?

3. Can congregational fundraising, even for an endowment, avoid competing with the regular giving of tithes and offerings? What are some ways this can be done?

4. What are the consequences of adopting a pastoral leave policy without first having a reliable source of funds available to assure that the policy will work?

5. Is it best for finances to dictate policy, or for policy to dictate finances? Does one approach assure success over the other? What are the issues?

6. What kind of vision would be necessary for an endowment to be successful in your congregation? What should be the first steps toward achieving this vision? Try writing a clearly stated objective that would be persuasive in encouraging the congregation's support.

7. When do the advantages of an endowment outweigh the challenges?

8. What is the first thing elders should do when an endowment to support the pastor's continuing professional development is being considered?

9. How can elders encourage others to contribute financially as an endowment becomes operational?

10. What is the difference between a congregational endowment and a savings account in a local bank dedicated to the same purpose? Does one require more oversight than the other? Should this be the deciding factor? Will others agree with you? What are the issues?

Planning for Tomorrow's Pastor

— 24 —

The Next Generation

Sharing what has been learned

Elders who have successfully planned for their pastor's personal and professional welfare, over time, will have had experiences of sufficient value to qualify them for even greater service to the church, both local and beyond. This new potential can be viewed as another elder opportunity to provide impact to the broader Church by sharing with others what has been learned. It also could be considered a new responsibility for a congregation that has received God's blessing as it prospered under the ministry of a vital pastor. There is a meaningful way for elders, pastor and a congregation to work together as they share their new strengths with others. For example, a congregation can conduct an internship program for young people who may be thinking about entering the ministry, or for those who have already made the decision. This is something that can be easily administered.

A pastoral internship can take several forms. It can be made available to a member of a congregation desiring to explore the pastoral ministry. It can be an opportunity for a seminary student to spend time getting acquainted with the workings of a local congregation under the guidance of an experienced pastor and elders. An internship can be a way of bringing a recent seminary graduate, or someone who is new to a denomination, into a congregation to gain experience and to be vetted prior to receiving a call to become a full-time pastor. Such a program can also be conducted cooperatively with a seminary as an integral part of a degree program, similar to academic internship opportunities provided by many higher education institutions. These are just a few options. Any one of them can be a way of serving the church locally or denominationally by providing a learning opportunity for future pastors. Two or more can be combined to become a uniquely innovative program. Regardless of the goals and objectives of an internship, the basic components, resource requirements and congregational commitments are similar.

Just as with any other congregational planning, strong leadership is the key. It will require some adjustment of time allocation within the local ministry, but with care this need not be an impediment. If done carefully, the presence of an intern can become an asset to a congregation. At the same time, there is the need to assure that the intern does not become a "gopher" (go for this; go for that) for the pastor, or for anyone else in the congregation, being expected to do things no one else wants to do.

Elders should take the lead. Planning for an internship should be neither an overwhelming nor mysterious assignment. The requirements should be little different than what the elders already have done as they helped their pastors with personal matters. That is, a plan must assure that the intern's personal needs are met in a manner that will not interfere with the learning experience.

The concept of a student internship could be foreign to a congregation. This presents a good opportunity for elders to help their pastors and congregations recognize how an internship can become an integral part of the local ministry. It has the potential for being viewed either as a unique extension of the local ministry—an opportunity—or as a burden not to be attempted. For the congregation with qualified leadership and available resources, I see it as more than an opportunity. I see it as an obligation. It should be accepted as an obligation by elders and congregations having been blessed with the positive results of successful congregational planning for the personal needs of their own pastors.

We often hear of missed opportunities. In this case, if this opportunity is ignored, it could easily become a missed obligation. Accepting this obligation will require a total commitment by elders, pastors and members alike, even beyond the modest financial commitment and pastoral and elder mentoring time required. It also will require less obvious things like a new tolerance for the preaching of an inexperienced intern; a person with whom members may not be acquainted accompanying the pastor during a home visit; and even the possibility of being asked to lend some personal household items to help with the intern's summer lodging necessities.

Most obvious for the pastor will be the need to make time available for intern mentoring, not a small task. An intern must not be given a list of things to do and then turned loose until the end-of-internship exit interview. If taken seriously, this commitment will require increased time away from family and some new responsibilities for the pastor, and likely for an elder or two.

I have always been quick to advise anyone taking on a new responsibility, in addition to those that already exist, that two options are possible: either existing responsibilities must be reduced to accommodate the new, or if this is not necessary, current responsibilities must be viewed as not constituting a full-time job. If the latter is true of a pastor, the congregation is not getting what it is already paying for. It must be acknowledged here, however, that a professional compensated by a salary, typically has a generous amount of time-use flexibility. Thus, new responsibilities often can be accommodated with a few little-noticed adjustments. The fact still remains that the adjustments will always be related to task and time. This cannot be avoided. This is reality. (If more is added to a full cup, it will overflow.) An internship must not become a burden on the pastor.

There always will be a price to pay for the time required for intern mentoring and for general internship oversight. This must be factored into the planning. It is a real, direct cost, however indirect it may appear. The key components of a successful internship are effective mentoring, a well-managed program and the intern's successful learning experience. These three factors are interdependent.

Using the simplest form of an internship as an example, and assuming that a member from within a congregation desires to pursue the pastoral ministry, the following criteria, procedural steps and selected examples of activities are suggested.

1. It is best that before an internship program is initiated, it has been included in the congregation's short and/or long-range plans.

2. A comprehensive plan for the proposed internship should prepared, complete with goals and objectives for both the intern and the congregation. It will be helpful if it is sufficiently generic so it will be applicable to future internships, but specific in such matters as financial and other required support resources, including space. A carefully prepared plan should include the flexibility to permit modification in response to the unique needs of each intern.

3. Mentoring obligations of pastors and elders should be determined before an internship begins.

4. Depending upon an intern's requirements and available resources, an internship can be of varying lengths; typically one summer, or a year.

5. An example of a goal and a few possible supporting objectives for a summer internship follow:

   Goal: An intern who has experienced the realities of a local pastorate, and has demonstrated new competencies related to the responsibilities of a pastor

   Objectives: By the conclusion of the internship, the intern will have accomplished the following.

   - Read two new books: one on a contemporary issue related to the Church; one addressing the learning abilities of elementary school-age children
   - Prepared and successfully delivered four children's messages during morning worship services
   - Attended each regular meeting of the elders
   - Preached at least four sermons, each of which has been recorded and then critiqued with the pastor-mentor for content, delivery style and effectiveness

   Suggestion: Note that these objectives are all stated as "performance *end-products*." It might be wise to have them become the basis for a pre-internship agreement with the prospective intern, thus avoiding future misunderstandings about purpose and expectations.

6. An intern's personal objectives should be reviewed carefully with the intern by the pastor and an elder, but eventually with all elders during an elder meeting. Objectives should be compatible with, and mutually reinforcing of the congregation's mission.

7. Some selected internship activities and responsibilities that have proven valuable are referenced below. Each will depend upon available time, scheduling conflicts, recommended frequency and coordination with internship objectives. The activities selected should be unique to each intern.

    - Attend elder meetings
    - Attend congregational committee meetings
    - Attend a congregational business meeting
    - Learn the roles of congregational officers
    - Accompany the pastor on home and hospital visits and to various meetings
    - Observe counseling sessions
    - Teach a Bible school class
    - Lead a Bible study
    - Participate in a summer Vacation Bible School program
    - Assist/preside during worship services
    - Prepare sermons
    - Preach occasionally (depending on the intern's qualifications and experience)
    - Prepare and deliver children's messages
    - Help with youth groups
    - Attend denominational committee and board meetings
    - Become acquainted with congregational and denominational standards

- Study denominational documents, related doctrinal matters and contemporary issues
- Prepare a paper on a matter of importance to the local congregation
- Meet informally with individual elders and deacons; become acquainted with their families
- Meet regularly with the pastor as mentor
- Receive periodic critiques of performance
- Become acquainted with relevant parachurch organizations
- Attend conferences related to the ministry
- Read assigned books and articles
- Interact socially with members of the congregation and the community

8. If an intern is married, opportunity for the spouse to spend time with the pastor's spouse is important.
9. It is likely that some type of intern financial support will be necessary. This can be accommodated in the form of a scholarship arrangement whereby modest compensation is provided in exchange for agreed-upon service to the congregation, above and beyond the contributions generated by the learning experience. There can be the typical "fellowship-type" arrangement, where the intern is provided a stipend that requires no specific service contribution, and the intern simply uses the money for personal expenses. This is a generally accepted arrangement typically found in similar situations within the higher learning community, so it should not be foreign to the intern.

From where should the funds to support an internship program come? As with most congregational financial needs, there are a number of possible sources: the annual budget; a special fundraising effort; a small grant from a third party; an internship underwritten by an individual; small gifts; or a combination of these sources. A less typical, yet very viable option is to incorporate the cost of the program into a congregation's endowment. This is especially appropriate when an internship program is intended to become permanent (See ch. 23, Assuring Permanent Funding).

An internship program need not be a financial burden for a congregation. The main direct cost is usually the modest stipend to assist the intern with personal expenses. If the intern should be from somewhere other than the local congregation, lodging expenses may be required. Both of these expenses can be shared, thus not creating an unmanageable or unrealistic burden on either the intern or the congregation. There will likely be additional incidental expenses such as may be required for resource materials, occasional meals and local travel. The total cost to the congregation should be modest as most internships are short-term events, not usually repeated every few months. Thus, they will impact the budget only during a few months of any fiscal year.

As with most planning where a cost is involved, some decisions are based upon the anticipated expenses compared to the benefits expected. This holds true when a congregation must decide on the wisdom of starting any new ministry. Internship costs to the congregation can be estimated with little difficulty, whereas the benefit to the congregation may be less easily assessed as it can be very subjective. Some persuasion may be necessary within the congregation to encourage acceptance of the internship as an extension of the congregation's ministry. The expected benefit to the intern should require less explanation. This is where elder commitment and leadership will be very helpful.

It should not be difficult for elders who have successfully provided for their pastor's personal welfare to prepare a compelling plan encouraging the congregation to sponsor internships. The biggest challenge may not be managing an internship, but helping the congregation recognize it as an obligation to share a local asset with the next generation of pastors. Use of the planning concepts presented in previous chapters will helpful.

I am convinced of the value of internships, whether they be in higher or vocational education or the work of the church. The experiences gained by an intern constitute a value-added academic commodity well beyond what can be learned in the classroom. With effective elder leadership, and with relatively modest use of dollars and time, a congregation can contribute immensely to the real world education of the next generation. Results of far greater value than the investment will have been produced. A noble task!

From Here to Reality

1. Do you believe your congregation would accept the idea that it has an obligation to share what it has learned over the years as it has responded to your pastor's personal needs? What might be some reactions? What are some ways resistance could be turned into support?

2. If you believe there is reason to begin an internship program, will you be able to make a persuasive case before your congregation toward this end? How will you proceed? What is the first thing you should do?

3. What can your elders do to prevent a student internship from becoming an unnecessary burden upon your pastor? In what ways can individual elders be of help to both pastor and intern?

4. Suggest ways you can share your "pastoral care" experiences with other elders and congregations throughout your denomination.

Beyond Planning

— 25 —

A Pastor's Testimony

Been there, done that

David McKay

Reverend McKay is a retired pastor in the Presbyterian Church in America (PCA). He is a graduate of Thiel College where he majored in history, and Gordon-Conwell Theological Seminary.

I am one of the older ministers in my Presbytery. I have been preaching regularly for forty-one years. On more than one occasion, one of the younger men of the Presbytery has approached me with a question. "Does preaching get easier as you get older and more experienced?" I certainly understand that question. Younger ministers, when they find themselves having to prepare a sermon virtually every week, feel frustrated that they have not been able to put enough time into study and preparation. Many go to bed Saturday night with a sense of anxiety that their prepared messages are not as good as they should be. They are hoping that the insecurities they feel will lessen as they grow older and have more experience. But, when someone asks me if preaching gets any easier, my typical response is, "Are you kidding?"

Granted, it has been a while since I have experienced "Saturday evening butterflies," but I know that I now spend more time on my sermon preparation than I did when I started out. I would like to think that my preaching is better, but preaching has not gotten easier.

I believe that there is great value in having the elders of a church encourage the minister to take a sabbatical on a regular basis. I can think of several benefits to the minister. I have used such time to go and minister to a mission team in Romania while the team leader was on furlough. I used sabbatical time to take my two grown sons on a father-son trip. That trip was the last time we have found the time to do so. I was able to spend extended time with my family. I was able to do reading that I normally cannot get to during the weekly routine the ministry involves. I am grateful for these things, but would contend that the main benefit of the sabbatical was that it helped my preaching.

I am a firm believer in the benefit of expository preaching. I once heard Dr. Walter Kaiser give this advice: "Preach topically once every five years, then repent!" If one is preaching through a book of the Bible, it takes a great deal of work to really get a handle on the main teaching contained therein. About twenty-three years ago, I think it was, I was teaching an adult Sunday School class on I Corinthians. I encouraged discussion in such classes. One gentleman repeatedly found in whatever passage we were studying, an occasion to criticize the President of the United States. I was not an admirer of the President, but found it hard to see how every part of that letter of Paul had application to him. That gave me occasion to reflect on whether I was being a "one note Johnny" in my preaching.

For most of last year, I preached through I Kings. The second half deals with the prophet Elijah. I read several books on the life of Elijah. I Kings ends with Elijah alive (not so his nemesis Ahab), but I decided to move into II Kings, where we find Elijah taken to heaven in chapter two. Most books on Elijah skip chapter one, which speaks of Elijah calling down fire on captains of fifty sent by Ahab's son. I do not know if the authors of these books didn't find much preaching material in that text, but as I studied it, I noticed that II Kings 1 is one of the Old Testament places where we find mention of "the angel of the LORD," a figure we are to see as a pre-incarnate manifestation of the second person of the Trinity. So, I developed the idea of how, just as Elijah appears with Moses on the Mount of Transfiguration to encourage Jesus before his "departure" (Luke 9), Jesus appeared to Elijah. I received many comments on this, but I was reminded of the importance of giving a great deal of study to the text. When did I give a lot of time to the study of I Kings? During my sabbatical, three years earlier, I had time to give to preliminary study, and as time went on, file away other ideas, illustrations, etc. I would have had difficulty finding enough time during my regular schedule.

Often, the regular weekly routine the minister finds himself dealing with does not allow adequate time for sermon preparation. When I was fresh out of seminary, I did church planting. We did not begin regular worship services for the first three months after my arrival. I soon found I had gained the respect of ministers in that Presbytery. On more than one occasion I received a phone call on Saturday asking me to fill in the next day, and these calls were not because the minister had become ill. One minister called at 10 p.m. and said, "I just couldn't get a sermon pulled together yet."

One may occasionally assume that sermon preparation is a fairly easy thing. I once asked my elders how long they thought it took me to prepare a message. One elder, whom I greatly respect, shocked me with his response, "Oh, I don't know, five hours?" I shocked him with my reply, "Double that at the least."

This is where the extra time afforded by a sabbatical is so beneficial. During my last sabbatical, I not only studied I Kings, but Ephesians, planning to get to it after I Kings. This study continues today. I have already prepared four messages from Ephesians 1. It was after finishing my fourth message that I remembered that I had preached through Ephesians twenty-eight years ago. Yet, as I looked through those messages, I was shocked to see how dissatisfied I now am with them. I doubt that I will use anything I had prepared then. Then, I had preached a dozen sermons on the entire book. Now, I expect to devote that amount to each chapter.

In my denomination, we refer to ministers as "teaching elders." I like that. But if we are going to teach and teach well, it requires time to study and be refreshed.

I should give some clarification here. I was asked to write "A Pastor's Testimony" concerning sabbaticals. Clearly, I can testify that they are beneficial, but I may not be the best one to talk on this subject. As I said, I have been in the ministry for forty-one years. I have had a grand total of two sabbaticals. The first was after I had served my church for twenty-two years. I was the one who brought it up and had to push hard to get it. I had been dropping hints for some time, but no one was picking them up! When the elders agreed to give me some time, there was a certain amount of resistance and reluctance. Again, that was after twenty-two years. Most ministers don't stay at one church that long.

The point which I really want to drive home is this: it would be far better for the elders of a church to take the initiative here, rather than leaving the minister feeling as though he had to ask. Some people find it easy to ask for things, others do not. I would encourage elders to be proactive, discussing sabbaticals with candidates. It would be good to have one particular elder take the lead in this area, contacting churches which have given sabbaticals, and then reporting back on the benefits learned by granting them.

— 26 —

Experience of a Pastor's Wife

The blessings of strong elders

Amy Holdeman

Amy Holdeman attended Duke University where she majored in developmental psychology "because I wanted to be a mother and understand my children's minds." This was followed by her graduate work in administration at the University of Notre Dame

"Yes, I need your help! Rich doesn't realize he needs rest this week. He won't ask for this Sunday off from preaching. Can the elders please make him take it off?"

That was my plea to one of our elders when Rich was about twelve weeks into his most recent series of treatments for the chronic form of leukemia he had been fighting for three years. During the fall of this year, he has been well enough to preach every week, even while traveling weekly to The Ohio State University Medical Center for treatment. But he and I each needed a break. I knew he would not ask for help. So, I did. And my very wonderful elders stepped into action. They didn't even ask Rich for his opinion on the matter!

That kind of care and leadership is typical of the elders under whose guidance I have been for the last twenty-five years. Our elders are mature, godly and hardworking, sacrificing a great deal to shepherd this flock of God's people.

I would never have guessed I would be a pastor's wife. My husband, Rich, was getting his PhD in Molecular, Cellular, and Developmental Biology at Indiana University. I thought he would end up as a professor somewhere, emphasizing teaching over research as I knew that's where his heart was. He loves to teach.

We moved to Indiana for Rich to pursue his graduate degree and soon became involved with a small congregation. It was exciting to be in a congregation having a new associate pastor and wife who were our ages. Both had deep roots in the denomination and were excited to see the church grow. They enlisted Rich and me in their plans for outreach and soon we were hosting Bible studies in our home, having folks over for meals on Sundays and generally learning what it meant to love the body of Christ. Our pastor and his wife were also integral in tying us into this unique little congregation of Christians in the midst of a very liberal, university town. We were blessed to watch them parent their four children before we had any of our own.

Within about two years of becoming members of the congregation, we were surprised to find that there was serious interest in having Rich to be elected an elder. He was only twenty-eight years old. But there was a need as the congregation had only two "provisional" elders at the time in addition to the pastor and associate pastor. The provisional elders had been appointed by the denomination because the congregation lacked the number of resident elders to continue as a viable congregation. We needed our own elders.

Rich was overwhelmingly elected elder, along with one other elder, so the church no longer needed provisional elders. Rich learned a great deal during those early days about leadership within the church. Our congregation was fairly gentle on its new elder. Rich could attend denominational meetings during that time because of the flexibility of his schedule. He spent time with older men in the congregation who had been elders earlier in their lives. Within about two years of Rich's election, the congregation was blessed with another new, young member who quickly was elected elder, and then a few years after that, another man about Rich's age was elected elder. We then had four resident elders and two pastors. In about six years, the congregation went from needing provisional leadership to having a very strong, relatively young group of elders. God provided elders who had the time and energy to invest in the church.

It was during those early years that Rich and I began to talk and pray about the idea of him being called into the pastorate. He finished the PhD in Biology less than a year after our first daughter, Maggie, was born. The University offered him a visiting lecturer position and he began doing research in a new lab. Because of our love for the congregation and how integrated into our community we felt, we were not ready to leave.

Our associate pastor accepted a call to serve as pastor in a northern Indiana congregation. As our congregation had prospered during his tenure, the elders thought continuing the two-pastor model would be beneficial. Financially it was feasible. We searched for a new associate pastor for the better part of a year, and even made one call that was not accepted. It was during those months that Rich, with the guidance of the other elders, decided he would like to formally begin seminary training. He started working part-time for the congregation, taking seminary classes from afar, then began on-site seminary classes the next year. The congregation paid for Rich to commute to Pittsburgh where the seminary was located. He took as many classes as he could pack into a Monday and a Tuesday morning. We quickly determined that commuting to get the degree was not going to work. Our second daughter, Grace, was now about two years old and we were busy with "life" in our community. Anne arrived a year later.

Our elders developed a plan to send our family to Pittsburgh for one academic year and the congregation readily agreed. The University even granted Rich a one-year leave of absence from his teaching position. During that school year Rich was able to complete a good portion of his seminary work. He also developed close relationships with the professors at the seminary who graciously agreed to work with him while he was back home—and this was in the days before real distance learning *via* the internet! By the next spring, Rich had completed his MDiv and was graduated by the seminary. Our congregation then called him to the pastorate to serve along with our pastor that spring.

Before Rich had gone to the seminary, the elders, working closely with the congregation and its finance committee, committed to increasing the pastors' compensation packages at a rate significantly greater than inflation. By the time Rich was called, not only had the pastors' pay been increased, but vacation time, conference allowances and pastors' expense accounts were also improved. But the very thoughtful and generous addition that was new to Rich's call was the inclusion of a sabbatical leave to be earned at the end of every sixth year of service to the congregation. Rich would be given six months off from church work with full pay! I think it was a first of its kind in the denomination. At that time, seven years seemed a long way away.

Our fourth daughter, Jane, arrived during those first few years of full-time pastoring for Rich. Life with our girls was very full and fun.

Time for a sabbatical came quickly. Rich was still teaching full-time at the University, having worked through many titles during the intervening years, finally and officially becoming a "Lecturer." The congregation continued in its strong support of Rich's teaching at the University, seeing it as a very powerful ministry to the community. Rich enjoys the classroom so much and is in constant contact with unbelievers, whether they are his colleagues or students. Many blessings in the form of people have come from Rich's association with the University, including one elder (Wes) and one deacon, both former students of Rich.

As we entered that year, we realized we didn't yet have a plan for a sabbatical. Our pastor had accepted a call to plant a church in Terre Haute. Rich was now pastoring alone and had been for two years. The congregation was also in the process of extending a call to a second pastor, a former Indiana University student who had become a member of the congregation during his undergraduate years. As he and his wife were set to arrive that same summer, having us gone didn't seem like a good plan. Also, because of Rich's teaching at the University it was not feasible for us to take the whole sabbatical at once. So, we began making plans to take half of the sabbatical the first year. Rich contacted a pastor of our denomination located in Northern Ireland to see if there was an empty pulpit that he could fill. Ballyclabber soon became our destination. The plan was beginning to take shape and the entire family was very excited, to say the least.

Then in a single day our world was turned upside down. After having his routine annual physical, Rich received a call from his doctor (Wes, that former student and now close friend and elder in our congregation), telling him he couldn't leave town that afternoon for a meeting until after he had seen an oncologist. His white blood cell count was significantly elevated. It quickly became clear that Rich had a form of chronic leukemia. Needless to say, the next few months were a blur and our plans to go to Northern Ireland were to be held very loosely.

The people of our congregation are truly an amazing bunch! During those first months after the diagnosis, we had people bringing meals, praying continuously and loving us as only people who really know you can love you. A gift card to one of our favorite restaurants would show up taped to our front door. A daughter would receive a card from an elder's wife. A young woman from the church would come over to play games with our daughters.

By early spring, Rich's doctors were in agreement that a two-month trip to the UK would be safe for him. His energy level was lagging and he was having a few strange problems associated with the leukemia, but as one of the doctors said, "There are doctors and hospitals in Ireland, too." So, in late May we left for eight weeks of what could only be called the most special time of our lives. Over the course of those weeks, we experienced exceptional hospitality, outrageous generosity, and saw some of the most beautiful parts of God's glorious creation. We came back from Northern Ireland a changed family.

The next six months were difficult for us as Rich went through traditional chemotherapy. The refreshment of the previous summer helped carry us through some very long months. The disease responded well to the treatment and Rich was pronounced "in remission." The Ballyclabber congregation made it clear they would love to have us back; so, the second half of Rich's sabbatical and another summer with our Irish "family" awaited us. When we arrived back in Northern Ireland, it was as if only a few days had passed. We settled back into our Irish life: church, farm, sightseeing day trips, picnics, meals with friends and ministering to a sweet group of saints one-third of the way around the world from our home. The second summer sabbatical passed even more quickly than the first.

Before developing strong opinions on a subject it is wise to gain experience. Twelve years into the pastorate and twenty-three years into church leadership for Rich is enough time for me, as wife and observer, to have developed some very strong opinions about what makes for "successful" and sustainable ministry. Elders have to take the "long view" of their ministry to a congregation. It is a marathon, not a sprint.

For the pastor, there tends to be more flexibility to a work day. Sleeping in after a late night meeting is sometimes a possibility. Eating lunch almost every day with your wife because much of your work is done from home during weekdays is a pleasure most husbands don't have. A pastor needs to fully embrace the 24/7 nature of the pastorate. There is no clocking in and out. There really are very few days "off." The blessing of flexibility should be appreciated fully!

One lesson Rich learned as a pastor is that it is essential to respect an elder's time. He is committed to leading efficient session meetings and making sure he is fully prepared for them beforehand. Elders usually have to go to their "real jobs" early the next day. An elder needs to know personal strengths and weaknesses as a leader in the church. Some elders are excellent Sunday school teachers and some aren't. Some elders are gifted at presiding over a worship service. Some are not. Most elders are able to effectively counsel the members of their church on personal matters. It is important for the long-term viability of an elder, that the elder not be put into situations that outstrip gifting. The time and energy required for an elder to faithfully attend monthly meetings and help shepherd the flock is tremendous.

The family of the elder should also be given a special measure of appreciation. Their husband and dad works all day then goes to meetings that seem to occur far too often and last far too long (especially to young children!). Our elders' families are all heavily involved in hospitality which helps to lighten the load on the pastors' families. I have told many people that I have been blessed with the best elders' wives imaginable. They manage their own homes well. They are raising their children faithfully in the fear and admonition of the Lord. They show incredible hospitality. I am inspired by them to do better because of my appreciation for their faithful service.

It really is a love fest around here. I cannot imagine being anywhere else. This place and these people have been used mightily by God in my life. I just pray they all know how much they are appreciated.

Afterword

I want to tell you about a small congregation and the change it has experienced during the last fifty years. Remarkable change! Spiritual change! And almost every other type of positive change imaginable. Change that could only have happened as a result of the Holy Spirit working through its leaders and members, then and now.

The congregation had been in existence for nearly one hundred and fifty years. Following years as a thriving congregation, membership declined. Pastors, seemingly viewed only as "preaching employees," remained for relatively short periods. Visionary leadership was lacking. The congregation appeared to have assumed an inward-looking survival mode. Spiritual lethargy was evident.

Much changed during the fifty years, but the change was very slow. I had a colleague who once said that, "If the Edsel had been a department in a university, it would still be in production." He meant that institutions of higher education are notoriously slow to make changes. He was correct. But I believe the church would usually win most slow-to-change contests.

In God's providence, this congregation called a pastor who served for over twenty years as a patient visionary and effective spiritual leader. He had a unique ability to see things others could not (or would not) see. His quiet but effective manner encouraged most of the elders to join in a plan for the future.

As time passed, due to deaths and relocation, only one resident elder remained causing the congregation to be perilously close to being reclassified by its denomination as only a mission station. However, two temporary elders were appointed by the denomination to avoid this possibility, each driving to monthly elder meetings; one from over sixty-five miles away, the other from approximately one hundred and twenty-five miles away.

Elder leadership was weak, at best. This was underscored by an emotional comment made by one of the members during a congregational meeting: "We need leadership!"—a jolt to the elders' ears. This cry for help coming from within this dormant congregation may have been an early turning point among the many yet to come. It actually served as encouragement, as it could not be missed that the congregation was wanting something to be done. The elders listened. They had received their marching orders.

A short-range plan was prepared by the elders and presented to the assembled congregation. It described the existing situation and proposed some steps to be taken toward what at the time seemed an unlikely future. It included graphic data describing the makeup of the membership. The average age of the members was approximately sixty years. Another graphic showed clearly that if the decline in membership continued, the congregation soon would be extinct. A longtime and respected member turned to the congregation and said, "If we don't do something now, we'll be gone." The plan was approved.

As finances were extremely limited, a second plan in the form of a grant proposal appealing to the larger denomination for assistance was successful in attracting a modest grant necessary to begin the first steps of the congregation's plan for the future. The proposal was preceded by an appeal by the elders to the membership for "above and beyond" giving. As a demonstration of commitment and leadership, a pledge was made by the pastor and each elder to also contribute beyond their regular tithes and offerings. This was called "Pacesetter Giving." Thus, the entire congregation had provided clear evidence to the denomination of tangible commitment to its own plan as presented in the request.

Members, previous members, friends of the congregation and members of other congregations were then invited to join the congregation at an anniversary dinner celebrating the congregation's one hundred and fiftieth year. This was also understood to be an opportunity for others to join the congregation by contributing financial gifts to help with plans for facility improvement.

God blessed these efforts. A third plan, including several goals and supporting objectives were developed by the elders and approved by the congregation. It was a work in progress, supported all along the way by the prayers of the elders, members, friends of the congregation and by prayers throughout the denomination. Fundraising was not the focus; careful planning and prayer was.

Over time, many changes occurred, but very slowly. This was good, as the congregation needed time to adjust to what was happening. The comfort of caring primarily for "ourselves" soon turned to an attitude of "what can we do for others?" A congregational task force called, "What Visitors See," took a careful look at what visitors' impressions might be as they entered the church building. Changes were made; even little things, like directions for finding a restroom. Some bigger things too, like upgrading sanctuary seating, lighting and the sound system; adding more helpful exterior signage; and expanding the library.

Not all was easy. Initially, there was some resistance to several aspects of the plans being developed, yet with patience and prayer, progress continued. The congregation became a welcoming congregation. As attendance and membership increased, so did the obvious vitality of the congregation. New voices contributed to enthusiastic and meaningful singing during worship services. New permanent elders were elected. Reflecting the developing concern for others, an Associate Pastor for Outreach was employed who served for several years before receiving a call to a nearby congregation. A new Associate Pastor was then employed, eventually also receiving and accepting a call to pastor another congregation. One of the elders, recognizing God's call to the ministry, was financially supported by the congregation as seminary studies were pursued. While studies were still ongoing, the elder was given the title, "Pastoral Associate" (a unique position and title created for a new and unique situation).

The pastor whom God had used so effectively in the congregation throughout these years of change, considering his work completed, moved on to a nearby community to start another congregation. The Pastoral Associate, after having been called as the congregation's second pastor, was then called to replace the departing pastor. A university student, who at the time was worshiping with the congregation, also became convicted of a call to the ministry. The congregation then supported this student while attending seminary prior to returning as the congregation's new second pastor. As complicated as these personnel changes may now appear, they each contributed immensely toward the revitalization plan God obviously had for this congregation. Confidence grew.

What was happening was being noticed by others. In time, the elders realized that the congregation had something to offer to other churches in the denomination, in addition to those who had been called from their midst to serve elsewhere as pastors, each in a nearby congregation. A very successful, well-attended national conference on the topic of church revitalization was held by the congregation. This was tangible evidence of the new-found confidence of a congregation wanting to share what it had learned through its experiences, and how it had received God's blessing along the way.

Today, over fifty years later, the congregation has been transformed from a near-death experience into a vibrant, growing and spiritually strong congregation. It now has two pastors and a summer pastoral intern program in place. Membership has more than doubled. New elders and deacons have been elected. The need for additional worship and classroom space has become a major problem—a good problem! The purchase of adjacent property (sold forty years ago because "we'll never need it") is being pursued for desired facility expansion. A balcony, vacant for many, many years, has been retrofitted to provide additional seating in a sanctuary now being filled to capacity.

A well-attended teaching program for all ages taught by the elders, pastors and others, precedes each worship service. Active Bible studies, prayer groups and other programs for all ages, youth through seniors, meet regularly. A week-long summer Vacation Bible School accompanies other neighborhood and community outreach initiatives; even an annual neighborhood "outreach" garage sale. New Mercy, Outreach, Missions, Facilities and Finance committees supplement the work of very busy elders, deacons and pastors. Social events abound. Members enthusiastically attend and participate in regional, national and international conferences and other denominational programs. Elders hold periodic retreats for reviewing current plans and setting new goals and objectives. Elder meeting agendas are experiencing an increase in issues that involve personal and family counsel, oversight, interviews for membership and an occasional discipline matter, each evidence of a growing congregation.

A new unity of purpose is evident. Members of the congregation have visited former members now residing in other states. Pastors have even made pastoral calls on other former members and adherents now living in foreign nations.

Significantly, a refreshingly new and very encouraging attitude toward its pastors began to appear over time. Pastoral compensations are now based upon qualifications, experience and performance; not time in place or the prevailing average wages of members. Budgets are being met and even exceeded. Elders have assured each of their pastors the support required to achieve and maintain a vital ministry. Provision is included in the congregation's policy and annual budget for the time and other resources required for its pastors to attend conferences, study, travel and take sabbatical leaves. The availability of personal time with family, in addition to vacations, has been encouraged, even assured.

Congregational policy encourages both the congregation and its pastors to be flexible and understanding when personal and pastoral responsibilities collide. To be certain that the pastors do not overcommit to the point of ignoring personal needs, including their own schedules and health, each month's activities and use of time are reviewed and discussed during regular elder meetings. Personal matters and suggestions for improving the ministry are reviewed at least annually.

There is little resemblance to the congregation of the past. I know this, as this congregation is my congregation. I have seen it all happen.

To God alone give glory.

"...I will build my church..."

Matthew 16:18

Acknowledgments

I would have found it impossible to have addressed all aspects of the topics I have included in the preceding chapters had I not had the insights and perspectives of others beyond my own. They have been places, done things and learned things that I have not.

Throughout what I have written, I have referenced observations made over the years, and a number of conclusions reached. Some have originated from within the church, others beyond the church. Many have involved people who do not and will never know that they have contributed. Several others would not want to be acknowledged here. Some for what they have said or done, others for what they have not said or done. Whoever and wherever they are, and whatever may have been the reason for my direct or implied references to them, each will be remembered for having contributed, even in absentia. Without these unsuspecting and forever anonymous contributors, what I have written would have been incomplete. To each I say thank you. If you are "listening," please accept this acknowledgement of your help, intentional or not.

Two contributors have each given freely of their time, their convictions, their talents and personal experiences, adding some reinforcing insights to what I have written. They must not remain anonymous. Each has earned my deepest appreciation, and deserve my special and unreserved acknowledgment here.

> **David McKay** has provided "A Pastor's Testimony" in response to my desire to have a "real live pastor" share what it is to have "been there and done that." Without hesitation he accepted my invitation to summarize his sabbatical experiences. He has helped to reinforce the importance of how the initiative of elders can be so very helpful to their pastors, especially those in mid-career.

Amy Holdeman, pastor's wife and mother of four daughters, graciously agreed to take some time from her extremely busy life to put the "experiential icing" on my "elder responsibility cake." In her typically enthusiastic fashion, she has shared the "Experience of a Pastor's Wife," something only one who is the "real deal" could have done.

My writing began by recognizing a need, knowing what I wanted to accomplish, but not being certain of how I could do it by myself. The generosity of these two very special contributors provided the answer, giving me increased confidence. You will note that what they have shared is presented at the end of what I have written. This has been intentional as each has helped me bring this book to a conclusion. They have, by example, provided evidence that elders can have an enormously positive impact upon the personal and professional lives of pastors, and upon the lives of their families. This has been my purpose. Thank you, David. Thank you, Amy.

There are others. In spite of a very full personal calendar, one who refused to say "no" when I asked if he would read and help me with my early drafts, is a former associate pastor, David Hanson. He has always kept an eye on me, even now from a distance. I'm thankful for the good memory and willingness of Bill Roberts, a former pastor, as he helped me with the accuracy of the historic content in my Afterword. Bob Brady, who has been a great encourager to me, also volunteered to guide me along the way by reviewing some of my early drafts, offering helpful criticism and ways to avoid literary potholes. And, of course, there is Ken Smith to whom I have dedicated this book. Ken was the one who really got me started, challenging me to write a paper on how the local church can benefit from the many illustrations of planning found in Scripture. The third chapter of this book is the result. He has also faithfully given me some essential pointers as I expanded upon his original challenge. These are all wonderful friends who recognized my work as one of passion, not profit.

And of course, there is my family. First, my wife, Jean, who I must assume was very happy to have me off in my study and out of the way while I wrote. However, she always rescued me cheerfully when I reappeared with an occasional grammatical question: she a former

English teacher, and I, a former inattentive eighth-grader during Miss Knowles' grammar lessons. Daughter Laurie "saved my life" on many occasions with her computing skills when my word processing needs extended far beyond my competence. And Cynthia, a daughter well-experienced in things philanthropic, helped me navigate some of the topics I encountered, including those related to congregational endowments. She also stepped in and rescued me from the tedium of reading and rereading my many drafts. I have a wonderfully supportive family to whom I remain incredibly indebted.

All of these very special people, even those remaining anonymous, have made my effort worthwhile. I trust others will agree.

WfM

The Author

Dr. Wendell McBurney is recognized for his commitment to spiritual revitalization based upon careful planning in the local church, and attention to the personal welfare of its pastors. He has demonstrated this by what he has written. There has been no other motive.

Dr. McBurney is a member of the Reformed Presbyterian Church of North America, having served his denomination for over fifty years as elder, preceded by eight years as deacon. He has been instrumental in the life of his congregation, helping its elders and pastors as they embarked upon a revitalization program that, with the Holy Spirit's leading and God's blessing, has resulted in new spiritual vitality and increased membership. An essential component of this program was the care given to the personal and professional needs of the pastors.

As Dean of Research and Sponsored Programs, and during his employment by Indiana University, Dr. McBurney was responsible for writing and reviewing grant applications and helping university faculty obtain federal, corporate and private funding for their research and other projects. He has been the recipient and project director of his own federally funded grants. His experience includes conducting proposal writing seminars and workshops for college and university faculty and administrators, civic, church and parachurch groups throughout the nation.

Following ten years of service on the school board of trustees in his community, including two terms as its president, Dr. McBurney became a founding director of the education foundation for the schools in the same corporation, serving as chair of its grants committee. He also served on the board of directors and as chair of the grants committee of the community foundation in his county.

As a member of his denomination's church revitalization committee, Dr. McBurney has been called upon to address planning and related issues for elders and other church leaders. He was helpful in assisting a theological seminary in attracting an approximately $1million grant to establish the Center for Pastoral Refreshment (CPR) on its campus. Dr. McBurney's experience occasionally advising pastors as they applied for sabbatical leave support, prompted him to make the same kind of help available to other pastors and their elders. Experience gained while assisting church and parachurch leaders with strategic and long-range planning, and his desire to help elders assume and demonstrate an increased attention to the personal needs of their pastors, has led him to encourage others to recognize the relationships among good planning, good pastoral care and vital churches.

Prior to his retirement, Dr. McBurney held a faculty appointment in the Indiana University School of Education, and adjunct appointments in the Indiana University Center on Philanthropy (now the Lilly Family School of Philanthropy) and in the Indiana University School of Public and Environmental Affairs wherc he taught graduate courses on proposal writing and grant management.

Dr. McBurney is a graduate of Geneva College, earning an undergraduate degree in the biological sciences. He holds the title of Trustee Emeritus from his alma mater. He completed his graduate studies in science education at Indiana University, and currently chairs a committee responsible for awarding scholarships to Indiana University students in the College of Arts and Sciences and the School of Education. He is a former president of the Indiana Academy of Science.

His non-academic and off-the-clock interests have included raising and showing prize winning poultry. He has been known to say that a good conversation with his geese served as therapeutic reprieve after a day of administrative conversations, contests and decision making. When not talking to his geese, time has been spent since childhood following trends in the world of "automobilia," from Tucker to Tesla.

Dr. McBurney and his wife are the parents of three adult children.

Made in the USA
Middletown, DE
17 September 2025

17006545R00130